Day Walks
South

20 circular routes
Hampshire & Sussex

Vertebrate Publishing, Sheffield
www.**v-publishing**.co.uk

Day Walks on the SouthDowns

20 circular routes in Hampshire & Sussex

Deirdre Huston

Day Walks on the SouthDowns

20 circular routes in
Hampshire & Sussex

 First published in 2011 by Vertebrate Publishing.
This second edition first published in 2020 by Vertebrate Publishing. Reprinted in 2021.

Vertebrate Publishing, Omega Court, 352 Cemetery Road,
Sheffield S11 8FT, United Kingdom.
www.v-publishing.co.uk

A CIP catalogue record for this book is available from the British Library.

ISBN 978-1-912560-91-2

Cover photo: Lullington Heath (route 19).
Back cover: View towards Arundel Castle from the Downs.
Photography by **Deirdre Huston** unless otherwise credited.

 All maps reproduced by permission of Ordnance Survey on behalf
of The Controller of Her Majesty's Stationery Office.
© Crown Copyright. 100025218

Design by Nathan Ryder, production by Jane Beagley.
www.**v-publishing**.co.uk

Printed and bound in Europe by Latitude Press.

Vertebrate Publishing is committed to printing on paper from sustainable sources.

MIX
Paper from
responsible sources
www.fsc.org FSC® C014138

Contents

Introduction vii
Acknowledgements viii
About the walks viii
Walk times viii
Navigation ix
Refreshments ix
South Downs National Park ix

Safety x
Lyme disease x
The Countryside Code xi
How to use this book xiv
Maps, descriptions, distances xv
Km/mile conversion chart xv
South Downs Area Map xvi

SECTION 1 – HAMPSHIRE

1 Cheriton: Well-trodden Paths & Civil War Battlefields – 13.8km/8.6miles 5
2 Winchester Hill Fort & the Meon Valley – 17km/10.6miles 11

SECTION 2 – WEST SUSSEX

3 An Enclave of Tranquility at Harting Downs – 15km/9.3miles 21
4 Explore Two Sides of a Beautiful Downland Valley – 12km/7.5miles 27
5 A Woodland Climb to Ancient Common & Heath – 13km/8miles 33
6 Black Down, Up High & Inspiring: Tennyson's Summer Home – 10.5km/6.5miles ... 39
7 Ancient Ebernoe Common & Milk Wood – 10.4km/6.5miles 45
8 River Arun & Easy Downland Loop – 14km/8.7miles 51
9 An Invigorating Hike to the Lee Side of the Downs – 18km/11miles 57
10 Historic Arun Floodplain – 22km/13.7miles 63
11 Chalk Escarpment, Distinctive Woodland & Chanctonbury Ring – 12.4km/7.7miles ... 73
12 Bramber and Beeding Hill: Town & Downland Loop – 12.6km/7.8miles 79
13 Spectacular Devil's Dyke Versus Secrets of Low-Lying Footpaths – 10.4km/6.5miles ... 85
14 The Heart of the Historic Downlands – 14km/8.7miles 91
15 Gateway to the Downs – 14.3km/8.9miles 99

SECTION 3 – EAST SUSSEX

16 Agricultural Weald, Pubs & Downland to Ditchling Beacon – 19.5km/12.1miles ... 111
17 Vistas over Lewes Rape – 14.5km/9miles 119
18 From Villages to Beacons, Ridges to Coach Roads – 13.3km/8.3miles 127
19 A Favourite Walk: Forest, Heath, Downland & Chalk Cliff – 22.6km/14miles 135
20 Heritage Coastline – 12km/7.5miles 143

APPENDIX 148

Introduction

Day Walks on the South Downs details 20 circular walks which will help you explore the South Downs National Park. Sections of deservedly popular trails such as the South Downs Way combine with lesser-known paths. These loops lead you past viewpoints and points of interest to convivial pubs and cafes, so that as you walk and relax, you can also discover history and observe nature.

Back in 2011, around the time it became a national park, I explored the South Downs for the first edition of this guidebook. I marched along ridges and clifftops, each new mile allowing expansive views to unfold. I persevered up chalk escarpments to claim forgotten ruins, desolate battlefields and quiet dewponds as my own. I navigated tree-covered slopes and tiptoed through grazing fields, as much watched as watching.

Through making short films, I have since explored the local history of Saddlescombe Farm (see Route 14, The Heart of the Historic Downlands) and wider areas of National Trust estates such as Cissbury Ring. Many rights of way which criss-cross the Downs are ancient routeways, and whether it is chalk, cobblestone or flattened grass underfoot, we can be certain of one thing – others have passed this way before us.

This year I returned to these trails and, once again, was struck by how spectacular the South Downs can be: the flicker of an adonis or chalkhill blue butterfly, shimmering grasses on a sunny day, chalky streams tumbling through ancient woodland, a heath where fragrant thyme and chalk flowers such as purple orchids grow among pink heathers.

Walking is about having the wind in your face, the sun in your eyes or the rain at your back. Enjoy reflective solitude amidst the peaceful South Downs or relish the simple pleasure of a walk with friends or family. Make time to stop at a friendly pub, choose a slice of cake at a cafe or picnic at a viewpoint.

Whatever walking means to you, I hope that you enjoy the walks in this guidebook and share my excitement in exploring the South Downs National Park.

It's all out there waiting for you! Who knows what you may discover?

Deirdre Huston

Acknowledgements

With love and thanks to Ian Rayland, for his unceasing support, unfailing sense of direction and boundless energy through many miles. Thanks to my father, Bob Huston, for continuing to share his love of the outdoors with all our family. I would also like to thank fellow walkers, friends and family who have accompanied me on days out to explore the South Downs: Carol Turner, Melody Staff, Sally Freeman and my children, Sean, Tegan and Rory xx.

About the walks

Most of the walks described here are between 6 and 14 miles and take about four to six hours to complete.

As with all walking keeping a close eye on the weather forecast will pay dividends, especially regarding cloud levels – the views and scenery are spectacular, but the going will sink into the 'Grey Gym' should the cloud come down. Apropos mist, most of the navigation here is simple, often following tracks, walls and fences, but a bit of map and compass work could be required at times, but this is flagged up in the walks.

The **summary** and route **description** for each walk should be studied carefully before setting out on a walk. Together they describe the terrain involved, the amount of ascent and the level of navigation skills required.

All the walks in this guide follow public rights of way or other routes with public access, including *permitted* or *concession* footpaths.

Walk times

The time given for each walk is on the generous side and based on a pace of around 4km per hour or 2 1/2 miles per hour, with time allowed for ascent and difficulty of terrain. There is some allowance for snack breaks and photo stops, but prolonged lunches should be added in.

Navigation

For most walks in this guide, following the route description in combination with the route map provided should be sufficient. However it is recommended you carry with you the appropriate map as a back up. The routes in this book are covered by the following maps:

Ordnance Survey Explorer OL8 Chichester (1:25,000)
Ordnance Survey Explorer OL10 Arundel & Pulborough (1:25,000)
Ordnance Survey Explorer OL11 Brighton & Hove (1:25,000)
Ordnance Survey Explorer OL25 Eastbourne & Beachy Head (1:25,000)
Ordnance Survey Explorer OL32 Winchester (1:25,000)
Ordnance Survey Explorer OL33 Haslemere & Petersfield (1:25,000)

A reasonable level of map reading ability and competence in the use of a compass is advised although not essential. If you possess a GPS (Global Postioning System) this can be a useful navigational aid in locating your position. However it is not a remedy for poor navigational skills.

Refreshments

A little research in advance of your walk can pay dividends. Tea rooms and kiosks may be seasonal or offer reduced opening hours. Rural pubs are usually not open all day and may only serve food at set times. At weekends, popular pubs increasingly require booking – worth doing even if your time is approximate. Take a back-up of sandwiches and plenty of water if unsure. Most pubs welcome muddy boots into bar areas.

South Downs National Park

The South Downs National Park came fully into being in 2011, the same year as the first edition of *Day Walks on the South Downs* was published. It covers a whopping 1,627 square kilometres (628 square miles) in southern England and takes in parts of Hampshire, West Sussex and East Sussex. The much-loved chalk hills of the South Downs, including the iconic white cliffs of the Seven Sisters and Beachy Head along the English Channel coast, are a well-known part of this national park but it also includes the western Weald, which is characterised by heavily wooded sandstone and clay hills and vales. The South Downs Way stretches all the way from Winchester to Eastbourne and is the only national trail to lie wholly within a national park. The walks in this guidebook often take in sections of the South Downs Way but also incorporate other less obvious but equally interesting places to explore.

Safety

It is strongly advised that appropriate footwear is used – walking boots or approach shoes designed to provide stability and security on uneven and slippery terrain. A waterproof, windproof jacket is essential and waterproof overtrousers or trousers are strongly recommended. Sufficient insulating clothing should also be worn or carried, that is appropriate to the type of walk planned and the time of year. Carry lots of food and drink, including an emergency supply. It's surprising how quickly you can become depleted and/ or dehydrated, especially at the end of the day.

Rescue

In case of an emergency dial **999** and ask for **Police** and then **Search and Rescue**. If you need the Coastguard, dial **999** or **112** and ask for the **Coastguard**. Where possible give a six-figure grid reference of your location or that of your casualty. If you don't have mobile reception try to attract the attention of others nearby. The standard distress signal is six short blasts on a whistle every minute.

Emergency rescue by SMS text

In the UK you can also contact the emergency services by SMS text – useful if you have low battery or intermittent signal. You need to register your phone first by texting **'register'** to **999** and then following the instructions in the reply. **Do it now** – it could save yours or someone else's life. **www.emergencysms.org.uk**

Lyme disease

An increasing problem, particularly bad in South-East England, and other areas populated by deer. It can affect a small number of people very seriously. Lyme disease is a bacterial infection that is spread to humans by infected ticks. Ticks are small, spider-shaped insects that feed on the blood of mammals, including humans. The most common symptom of Lyme disease is a red skin rash that looks similar to a bullseye on a dart board. Left untreated, other symptoms can develop, including: a high temperature (fever); muscle pain; joint pain and swelling; neurological symptoms, such as temporary paralysis of the facial muscles. A person with Lyme disease is not contagious because the infection can only be spread by the ticks. It's important to visit your doctor if you have been bitten by tick and you have flu-like symptoms: you are at risk as it can be difficult to diagnose it correctly. Visit **www.nhs.uk** for more information.

The Countryside Code

Respect other people

Please respect the local community and other people using the outdoors. Remember your actions can affect people's lives and livelihoods.

Consider the local community and other people enjoying the outdoors

» Respect the needs of local people and visitors alike – for example, don't block gateways, driveways or other paths with your vehicle.

» When riding a bike or driving a vehicle, slow down or stop for horses, walkers and farm animals and give them plenty of room. By law, cyclists must give way to walkers and horse riders on bridleways.

» Co-operate with people at work in the countryside. For example, keep out of the way when farm animals are being gathered or moved and follow directions from the farmer.

» Busy traffic on small country roads can be unpleasant and dangerous to local people, visitors and wildlife – so slow down and where possible, leave your vehicle at home, consider sharing lifts and use alternatives such as public transport or cycling. For public transport information, phone Traveline on 0871 200 22 33 or visit **www.traveline.info**

Leave gates and property as you find them and follow paths unless wider access is available

» A farmer will normally close gates to keep farm animals in, but may sometimes leave them open so the animals can reach food and water. Leave gates as you find them or follow instructions on signs. When in a group, make sure the last person knows how to leave the gates.

» Follow paths unless wider access is available, such as on open country or registered common land (known as 'open access land').

» If you think a sign is illegal or misleading such as a *Private – No Entry* sign on a public path, contact the local authority.

» Leave machinery and farm animals alone – don't interfere with animals even if you think they're in distress. Try to alert the farmer instead.

» Use gates, stiles or gaps in field boundaries if you can – climbing over walls, hedges and fences can damage them and increase the risk of farm animals escaping.

» Our heritage matters to all of us – be careful not to disturb ruins and historic sites.

Protect the natural environment

We all have a responsibility to protect the countryside now and for future generations, so make sure you don't harm animals, birds, plants or trees and try to leave no trace of your visit. When out with your dog make sure it is not a danger or nuisance to farm animals, horses, wildlife or other people.

Leave no trace of your visit and take your litter home

» Protecting the natural environment means taking special care not to damage, destroy or remove features such as rocks, plants and trees. They provide homes and food for wildlife, and add to everybody's enjoyment of the countryside.

» Litter and leftover food doesn't just spoil the beauty of the countryside, it can be dangerous to wildlife and farm animals – so take your litter home with you. Dropping litter and dumping rubbish are criminal offences.

» Fires can be as devastating to wildlife and habitats as they are to people and property – so be careful with naked flames and cigarettes at any time of the year. Sometimes, controlled fires are used to manage vegetation, particularly on heaths and moors between 1 October and 15 April, but if a fire appears to be unattended then report it by calling **999**.

Keep dogs under effective control

When you take your dog into the outdoors, always ensure it does not disturb wildlife, farm animals, horses or other people by keeping it under effective control. This means that you:
» keep your dog on a lead, or
» keep it in sight at all times, be aware of what it's doing and be confident it will return to you promptly on command
» ensure it does not stray off the path or area where you have a right of access

Special dog rules may apply in particular situations, so always look out for local signs – for example:
» dogs may be banned from certain areas that people use, or there may be restrictions, byelaws or control orders limiting where they can go
» the access rights that normally apply to open country and registered common land (known as 'open access' land) require dogs to be kept on a short lead between 1 March and 31 July, to help protect ground nesting birds, and all year round near farm animals

» at the coast, there may also be some local restrictions to require dogs to be kept on a short lead during the bird breeding season, and to prevent disturbance to flocks of resting and feeding birds during other times of year

It's always good practice (and a legal requirement on 'open access' land) to keep your dog on a lead around farm animals and horses, for your own safety and for the welfare of the animals. A farmer may shoot a dog which is attacking or chasing farm animals without being liable to compensate the dog's owner.

However, if cattle or horses chase you and your dog, it is safer to let your dog off the lead – don't risk getting hurt by trying to protect it. Your dog will be much safer if you let it run away from a farm animal in these circumstances and so will you.

Everyone knows how unpleasant dog mess is and it can cause infections, so always clean up after your dog and get rid of the mess responsibly – 'bag it and bin it'. Make sure your dog is wormed regularly to protect it, other animals and people.

Enjoy the outdoors
Even when going out locally, it's best to get the latest information about where and when you can go. For example, your rights to go onto some areas of open access land and coastal land may be restricted in particular places at particular times. Find out as much as you can about where you are going, plan ahead and follow advice and local signs.

Plan ahead and be prepared
You'll get more from your visit if you refer to up-to-date maps or guidebooks and websites before you go. Visit **www.gov.uk/natural-england** or contact local information centres or libraries for a list of outdoor recreation groups offering advice on specialist activities.

You're responsible for your own safety and for others in your care – especially children – so be prepared for natural hazards, changes in weather and other events. Wild animals, farm animals and horses can behave unpredictably if you get too close, especially if they're with their young - so give them plenty of space.

Check weather forecasts before you leave. Conditions can change rapidly especially on mountains and along the coast, so don't be afraid to turn back. When visiting the coast check for tide times on **www.ukho.gov.uk/easytide** – don't risk getting cut off by rising tides and take care on slippery rocks and seaweed.

Part of the appeal of the countryside is that you can get away from it all. You may not see anyone for hours, and there are many places without clear mobile phone signals, so let someone else know where you're going and when you expect to return.

Follow advice and local signs
England has about 190,000km (118,000 miles) of public rights of way, providing many opportunities to enjoy the natural environment. Get to know the signs and symbols used in the countryside to show paths and open countryside.

How to use this book
This book should provide you with all of the information that you need for an enjoyable, trouble free and successful walk. The following tips should also be of help:

1. We strongly recommend that you invest in the maps listed above on page ix. These are essential even if you are familiar with the area – you may need to cut short the walk or take an alternative route.

2. Choose your route. Consider the time you have available and the abilities/level of experience of all of members of your party – then read the Safety section of this guide.

3. We recommend that you study the route description carefully before setting off. Cross-reference this to your map so that you've got a good sense of general orientation in case you need an alternative route. Make sure that you are familiar with the symbols used on the maps.

4. Get outdoors and enjoy walking!

Maps, descriptions, distances

While every effort has been made to maintain accuracy within the maps and descriptions in this guide, we have had to process a vast amount of information and we are unable to guarantee that every single detail is correct. Please exercise caution if a direction appears at odds with the route on the map. If in doubt, a comparison between the route, the description and a quick cross-reference with your map (along with a bit of common sense) should help ensure that you're on the right track.

Note that distances have been measured off the map, and map distances rarely coincide 100% with distances on the ground. Please treat stated distances as a guideline only. Ordnance Survey maps are the most commonly used, are easy to read and many people are happy using them. If you're not familiar with OS maps and are unsure of what the symbols mean, you can download a free OS 1:25,000 map legend from **www.ordnancesurvey.co.uk**

Here are a few of the symbols and abbreviations we use on the maps and in our directions:

 ROUTE STARTING POINT   ROUTE MARKER  OPTIONAL ROUTE

 ADDITIONAL GRID LINE NUMBERS TO AID NAVIGATION  SHORT CUT ROUTE

PB = public bridleway; **PF** = public footpath; **GR** = grid reference.

Km/mile conversion chart

METRIC TO IMPERIAL

1 kilometre [km]	1000 m	0.6214 mile
1 metre [m]	100 cm	1.0936 yd
1 centimetre [cm]	10 mm	0.3937 in
1 millimetre [mm]		0.03937 in

IMPERIAL TO METRIC

1 mile	1760 yd	1.6093 km
1 yard [yd]	3 ft	0.9144 m
1 foot [ft]	12 in	0.3048 m
1 inch [in]		2.54 cm

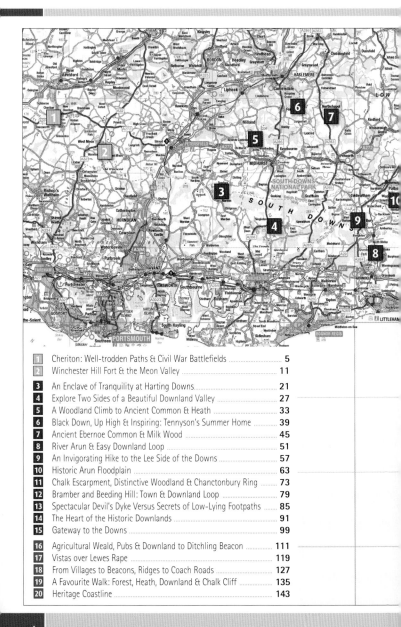

1	Cheriton: Well-trodden Paths & Civil War Battlefields	5
2	Winchester Hill Fort & the Meon Valley	11
3	An Enclave of Tranquility at Harting Downs	21
4	Explore Two Sides of a Beautiful Downland Valley	27
5	A Woodland Climb to Ancient Common & Heath	33
6	Black Down, Up High & Inspiring: Tennyson's Summer Home	39
7	Ancient Eberneoe Common & Milk Wood	45
8	River Arun & Easy Downland Loop	51
9	An Invigorating Hike to the Lee Side of the Downs	57
10	Historic Arun Floodplain	63
11	Chalk Escarpment, Distinctive Woodland & Chanctonbury Ring	73
12	Bramber and Beeding Hill: Town & Downland Loop	79
13	Spectacular Devil's Dyke Versus Secrets of Low-Lying Footpaths	85
14	The Heart of the Historic Downlands	91
15	Gateway to the Downs	99
16	Agricultural Weald, Pubs & Downland to Ditchling Beacon	111
17	Vistas over Lewes Rape	119
18	From Villages to Beacons, Ridges to Coach Roads	127
19	A Favourite Walk: Forest, Heath, Downland & Chalk Cliff	135
20	Heritage Coastline	143

Day Walks on the
SouthDowns
Area Map & Route Finder

SECTION 1

Hampshire

The serene atmosphere can be deceptive!
Look beyond the present and this area
is rich in history. Let low-rolling downland
and well-trodden paths lead you through
valleys and up slopes to hill forts
and battlefields. Look out for red kites
swooping over peaceful farmland too.

A FARM TRACK THROUGH HAMPSHIRE'S LOW-ROLLING DOWNLAND

CHERITON: WELL-TRODDEN PATHS & CIVIL WAR BATTLEFIELDS

DISTANCE: 13.8KM/8.6MILES » **TOTAL ASCENT:** 204M/669FT » **START GR:** SU 583284 » **TIME:** ALLOW 5-6 HOURS
SATNAV: SO24 0PZ » **MAP:** OS EXPLORER OL32, WINCHESTER, 1:25,000 » **REFRESHMENTS:** THE FLOWER POTS INN OR THE
HINTON ARMS, CHERITON; THE MILBURY'S, BEAUWORTH; THE TUCK SHOP, HOLDEN FARM CAMPSITE (SEASONAL
OPENING) » **NAVIGATION:** STRAIGHTFORWARD.

Cheriton: Well-trodden Paths & Civil War Battlefields

13.8km/8.6miles

An easy walk from the pretty village of Cheriton through rolling downland taking in a historic pub, Hinton Ampner and areas of the Cheriton Civil War Battlefield.

Cheriton » Mill Barrows nr Beauworth » Kilmeston » Hinton Ampner » Upper Lamborough Lane » Cheriton

Start

The war memorial on the village green in Cheriton. Roadside parking. GR: SU 583284.

The Walk

The village of Cheriton offers a charming mix of thatched cottages, a village green, a gentle stream and plenty of ducks! Meander out of the village to explore rolling downland on farm tracks. Join the South Downs Way and make the gentle climb to Milbarrow Down and the friendly Milbury's free house. The 400-year-old building sits beside an intersection of historic pathways.

Milbarrow Down was a Bronze Age barrow cemetery and a barrow mound can be seen above the crossroads. Itself unspectacular, the background makes it more than interesting. Bronze Age barrow mounds are primarily burial places for individuals rather than communal burials like earlier long barrows. An important person could have been buried here, kept company by a collection of material possessions to indicate their importance. Alternatively, was this a non-burial barrow, intended to mark territory on the highly visible hilltop horizon where the resulting mound of fresh chalk would be a striking landmark?

Follow the Wayfarers Walk across fields, through Kilmeston and on towards Hinton Ampner (National Trust). We approach the house from the south, a simple way to appreciate the position and outlook of this garden, known for its stunning views. Explore the thirteenth century church or detour to see the elegant interior of the house and wander through its gardens to intimately appraise Ralph Dutton's accomplished mix of formal and informal planting.

Beyond the A272, our route joins a section of the Cheriton Battlefield Walk. On 29 March 1644, the Battle of Cheriton decided the course of the Civil War in Southern England. Signposts have now seen better days but there are boards that point out where skirmishes between Royalists and Parliamentarians bloodied the landscape. We follow part of it, but if you want to divert to explore it more fully, please do so using the information boards and the optional route marked on our map. The sunken paths and lie of the land make it easy to imagine emotions and atmosphere as the battle unfolds.

01 CHERITON

Directions – Cheriton

➏ From the war memorial, follow the road past the parish hall. Walk along over the stream and **turn left** along Hill Houses Lane. Walk to the very end, past houses, to where the tarmac stops and continue along the mud byway.

2 At the fork, **continue straight ahead**.

3 At the wooden waymarker before the barn, **walk left** down the byway (Honey Lane). **Head right** at the signpost and soon pass through a gate.

4 Go **straight ahead** to take the lower track and join the South Downs Way (SDW). **Go left** through the gate, still following the SDW. Cross the A272 and follow the SDW through Holden Farm. At the barn, join the lane to make gradual climb **straight ahead** along the SDW.

5 **Walk right** up the lane following the SDW. Pass The Milbury's. **Turn left** at the crossroads following the SDW towards West Meon. (Look right beyond the hedge to see Bronze Age Mill Barrows.) Pass the entrance to Preshaw House. Cross to the left side and join narrow SDW track past the signpost as it runs **parallel** to the road.

6 **Turn left** leaving the SDW to follow the Wayfarers Walk where the track rejoins the road. Walk down the hill along the edge of the field to the stile. Continue straight ahead across the next field and go through the gap in the hedge, following the path straight ahead through the crop field. At the far side, look for the wooden waymarker on your right to lead you on to a 'hidden' footpath between the hedge and the fence. Pass a kissing gate and continue along the fence. Go through another kissing gate, across the field and through one last kissing gate.

7 You are now in Kilmeston, opposite the village hall. **Walk across the road and straight ahead**, following the road to Dean House. **Turn left** at the wooden signpost following the Wayfarers Walk. Go through a double gate and walk along a wooded path. Cross another couple of stiles and follow the line of the telegraph poles **straight ahead** to the far side of the field. Pass the church on your left and cross the stile.

8   **Walk right, and then immediately left, across a stile,** still following the Wayfarers Walk. You are passing Kilmeston Manor, but soon this will be dwarfed by the sight of the National Trust house Hinton Ampner. Walk through the gap and head straight on towards the gate.

9   **Walk straight ahead** through the gate. This fenced path runs through the grounds of Hinton Ampner. Follow the Wayfarers Walk through the gate. Pass the entrance to the church and the drive to Hinton Ampner. **Head right** through the gates to continue on our walk. Follow the road **straight ahead**.

10   Cross the A272 and follow the Wayfarers Walk on the concrete byway. See the Cheriton Battlefield Walk notice board (point 2).

11   **Walk straight ahead** at the crossroads of grassy tracks. Climb the slope. Probably not a welcome hill at this point but at least you're not a soldier at battle.

> **OR**   **Turn right** at the next crossroads, along the Cheriton Lane track to follow the Cheriton Battle Walk more fully, rejoining at point 12 below.

12   **Turn left** at Upper Lamborough Lane, still following the Wayfarers Walk. At the next path intersection, **turn left** to head downhill as we stay on the Battlefield Walk. At the signpost, **walk right** along the byway beside the fence, following the 'sunken' path. Don't miss point 4 of the Cheriton Battlefield Walk.

13   Cross the road and **turn right** to follow the pavement back into Cheriton, walking alongside the River Itchen.

WINCHESTER HILL FORT & THE MEON VALLEY

DISTANCE: 17KM/10.6MILES » **TOTAL ASCENT:** 380M/1,247FT » **START GR:** SU 677222 » **TIME:** ALLOW 5 HOURS
SATNAV: GU32 1PF » **MAP:** OS EXPLORER OL32 WINCHESTER, 1:25,000 » **REFRESHMENTS:** YE OLDE GEORGE INN OR IZAAK
WALTON, EAST MEON; SEASONAL CAFÉ, MEON SPRINGS; THOMAS LORD, WEST MEON » **NAVIGATION:** WELL-SIGNED EXCEPT
DURING WOODLAND STRETCH BETWEEN WESTBURY AND DRAYTON.

WILD FLOWERS ON WINCHESTER HILL

Winchester Hill Fort & the Meon Valley   17km/10.6miles

A steady climb to Old Winchester Hill and a leisurely meander through the luscious Meon Valley.

East Meon » Meon Springs » Old Winchester Hill » Meon Valley Trail » West Meon » Westbury Park » Drayton » East Meon

Start

Car park in East Meon, signed from the village centre. GR: SU 677222.

The Walk

Join the South Downs Way (SDW) to meander through the agricultural valley around East Meon. Look out for red kites swooping and gliding over the crop fields. Pass the fishery at tranquil Meon Springs, where a bacon roll on the cafe balcony might prove tempting.

Begin the steady and not too arduous climb to Old Winchester Hill, a place which retains atmosphere despite attracting 'honeypot' swarms. Most visitors stick to the hill fort trail so the outlying footpaths are surprisingly empty. Approaching on foot is a great way to gain a sense of its importance, topography and history. At the summit, the SDW has been re-routed, but detour to look at the early Bronze Age hill fort, believed to have been the settlement of a Celtic chieftain. Four flint and chalk barrow tumuli are preserved along the top of the ridge. Around 3,800 years ago, they stood out as brilliant white markers on the skyline.

Some smaller hollows date from a WWII mortar firing range. There is a trig point too and the site is a nature reserve, superbly managed by Natural England who encourage banks of wild flowers to flourish. We paused to watch a hunting hawk but you may also want to look out for various orchids, field fleawort and ox-eye daisies. During summer butterflies such as chalkhill blue own the hill.

Descend on Monarch's Way, climbing back up the valley before joining the flat, easy Meon Valley Trail. This runs along the disused railway line to West Meon, where the churchyard boasts occupants such as the spy, Guy Burgess, and Thomas Lord, founder of the cricket ground. You may prefer to visit Thomas Lord, the pub, with its large garden and good reputation for food! A final, contrasting section leads you through broadleaf woodland with a woodpecker soundtrack and some big old trees. Then home across the fields to the thatched village of East Meon and its welcoming pubs.

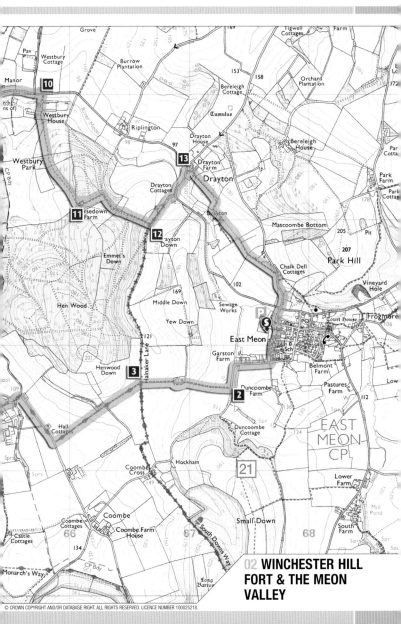

02 WINCHESTER HILL FORT & THE MEON VALLEY

Directions – Winchester Hill Fort
& the Meon Valley

❻➡ Take the footpath opposite the car park. Go across the field, through houses and **bear right**, following the road. At the top of Duncombe Road, **go right** along the lane.

2 **Turn right** along footpath towards 'Forty Acres'. Keep left at the farm and continue down through the field past a (broken) signpost.

3 At path crossroads, go **straight ahead**, joining the South Downs Way (SDW) to Meonstoke. At the lane, **turn right** then at Meon Springs Fishery, **turn left** still following the SDW. **Turn right** after the flint barn. By the disused chalk pit **bear right** on to the steep-ish climb.

4 Go through the gate to Old Winchester Hill lay-by. Follow the SDW **left** alongside the lane. Towards the top, cross the road to continue on the SDW.

5 Detour to explore Old Winchester Hill Fort, a Bronze Age site, nature reserve and viewpoint. Afterwards **go left** to follow the re-routed SDW as it skirts around the fort. Steep descent. **Turn right**. Ignore the footpath heading right back to the fort and instead **continue straight ahead** and follow path right. After the field, follow the SDW **right and then left** at a junction.

6 Follow Monarch's Way **right** where the field slopes downwards (the wooden waymarker is partially obscured). Join a farm track near Roll's Copse and walk **straight ahead**. By the entrance to Peake Farm, follow the footpath **right** round the edge of the field. Go **left** briefly on a lane and then **right**, still following Monarch's Way. Pass the riding school and walk **left** on footpath.

7 **Turn right** for a steep, steady climb up the stony lane. At Hayden Lane, **turn left**.

8 **Walk right** after the bridge to join the footpath **above** the Meon Valley Trail. The path soon forks: go down **right** to leave the footpath and join the Meon Valley Trail. Go through the car park and along the drive to leave the Meon Valley Trail. **Turn left** at the lane and immediately **right** at the footpath opposite. Follow it round across the footbridge.

9 At the road, **walk left** to explore West Meon village and/or pub, or **go right** to continue on route. Short, unavoidable stretch along the road, but there's some pavement. Pass Coombe Lane.

10 **Go right** on the signed (obscured) footpath at Westbury House. Follow the footpath **straight ahead** up the slope, past the marker post and through the gate. Follow the unmarked, winding track through the woods. At the small clearing, keep going in the **same direction**, **heading left through and then along the edge of the trees**.

11 At Horsedown Farm, go **left** through the waymarked gate to follow the footpath round. Go straight across a driveway and, at the field, **walk left** at the marker post along the grass track. At the lane, **go right**. The next turn-off is **easy to miss**: where the stony lane curves and begins to climb upwards, leave it to go **straight ahead** on the footpath. Almost immediately, come to a stile. Walk **right**, making the steep descent and crossing several stiles.

12 **Walk left** along the flint and mud byway. Join Halnaker Lane **straight ahead**. At the T-junction, **go left** for short way on the lane.

13 **Go right** along the signed, narrow footpath before Drayton Farm Barns. Go through the kissing gate and walk **straight ahead** through the metal gate. Grassy climb to a gate. Walk **straight ahead** through a crop field to a waymarked gate. Continue up the hill. Go through a kissing gate. See East Meon ahead and follow path **straight ahead**. Negotiate one last kissing gate and **go right** at the lane for East Meon, **straight ahead** at crossroads and **turn right** into the car park.

SECTION 2

West Sussex

The high drama of the Downs offers small pockets of wildness in the central area with rugged steep-sided escarpments, ridges and valleys. Enjoy too the peace of grazing fields and farmland, chalky woods and riverbanks, marshes and breathtaking nature reserves. Moving westwards, the Downs become much more wooded and there are ancient commons and milk wood waiting to be explored.

VIEW OVER SOUTH HARTING FROM HARTING DOWNS

03 An Enclave of Tranquility at Harting Downs

15km/9.3miles

A spectacular section of the South Downs Way with an undulating downland loop which leads you straight past the little-known ruins of medieval Monkton Farm and a tucked-away country pub, to return by easy, gently climbing bridleways.

Harting Hill » Beacon Hill » Pen Hill » Philliswood Down » Monkton Farm » Chilgrove » Hooksway » Little Round Down » Bramshott Bottom » Harting Downs » Harting Hill

Start

Harting Down Car Park on the B2141 between South Harting and Mid Lavant, near Chichester. GR: SU 790181.

The Walk

We start high with a beautiful section of the South Downs Way (SDW). The views are spectacular: the green copper spire of South Harting Church stands out against the agricultural backdrop. The ancient chalk downland of Harting Down (National Trust owned, nature reserve and SSSI) boasts a wide variety of plants and invertebrates. Look for evidence of Iron Age land formations: a fort on Beacon Hill and cross-dykes on Harting Down and Pen Hill. The notably steep climb up Beacon Hill can be avoided with a simple detour if necessary but the panorama from the trig and orientation points should tempt you onwards and upwards.

As you climb through West Dean Estate, look out for the moving shrine to a young German WWII pilot who crashed towards the top of the wooded hill.

A quick march down farm lanes brings you to The White Horse. Even if you're not planning to stop, the extensive terrace and wafts of the aroma of cooked lunches may tempt you. If you are in time to hit its opening hours, you may prefer to push on to the Royal Oak at Hooksway where you can share the fireplace with the ghost of William 'Shagger' Shepherd, a sheep rustler who was chased here and murdered by angry farmers.

Pleasant bridleways lead you back to the SDW and Harting Hill. It's worth mentioning that South Harting is where Belloc's characters in 'The Four Men: A Farrago' finish their four day, ninety mile trek across Sussex, so you are, perhaps, in good company.

AN ENCLAVE OF TRANQUILITY AT HARTING DOWNS

DISTANCE: 15KM/9.3MILES » TOTAL ASCENT: 433M/1,421FT » START GR: SU 790181 » TIME: ALLOW 6-7 HOURS SATNAV: GU31 5PN » MAP: OS EXPLORER OL8, CHICHESTER, 1:25,000 » REFRESHMENTS: THE WHITE HORSE, CHILGROVE, OR ROYAL OAK, HOOKSWAY » NAVIGATION: CARE NEEDED AFTER LEAVING SOUTH DOWNS WAY TO CORRECTLY FOLLOW FOOTPATH RIGHT OUT OF FIELD TOWARDS MONKTON FARM.

CROSS-DYKES ON PEN HILL

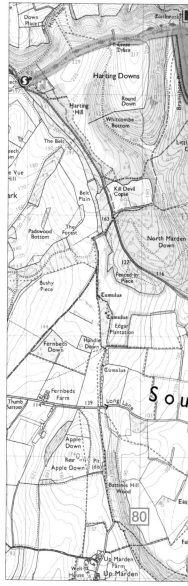

03 AN ENCLAVE OF TRANQUILITY AT HARTING DOWNS

Directions – An Enclave of Tranquility at Harting Downs

➔ From the car park, walk up along the bridleway to the five-bar gate. Go through the gate and veer left to join the lower parallel track beside the National Trust sign and follow the path. This is the South Downs Way (SDW). Follow the waymarkers **straight ahead. Watch your descent on Harting Down: extremely slippery compacted chalk.**

2 At Bramshott Bottom, by the five-way marker post, leave the SDW to go **straight ahead** up Beacon Hill.

> **OR** To avoid a steep climb, follow the SDW **right** and then **left** again before reaching Telegraph House, rejoining main route at point 3 by the gate in the valley between Beacon Hill and Pen Hill.

At the top of Beacon Hill, go through the gate and walk **straight ahead** to the trig point and orientation plate. Continue east: **straight ahead** down the hill on the bridleway past the tree plantation.

3 Re-join the SDW and walk **straight ahead** up the hill. At the top of Pen Hill, go through a gate and walk **straight ahead** curving left as you go down the hill. Near the base of the hill, follow the bridleway marker post left. At the next marker post, where the footpath joins the SDW, **turn right.**

At the junction with the byway, go **straight ahead**. Ignore a gate. Follow the SDW **right** at the fork by the wooden waymarker sign. **Turn left and immediately right** at signed junctions staying on SDW. Stay on the track as it wends its way through the trees.

4 Follow arrow on marker post **straight ahead** out on to the open grazing field. Walk along this undulating track, **turning right** at a marker post and climbing over a stile.

5 Reach a flint outbuilding by a three-way signpost and continue **straight on** along this footpath through West Dean Estate as it veers right up the hill. Pass through a gate and coppiced wood. Continue along this flinty track, it certainly has a historic feel.

6 **Turn right** near the cottage and walk along the lane. Ignore all footpaths and stay on the undulating lane until you reach The White Horse and the B2141.

7 At the B2141, **turn right** and walk along the grass verge for a short distance only. Follow the footpath through a gap by a signpost and walk roughly parallel with the road along the line of the fence. Go through a kissing gate and walk **straight ahead** along the footpath. Cross a driveway and go through a kissing gate and continue **straight ahead**.

Go **through a kissing gate** and walk **right** along the signed bridleway. This stony track can be muddy. The path becomes more flinty and passes through a gateway. When you come to two gates side-by-side, take the left-hand gate to walk along the bridleway through West Dean Estate. Continue **straight on** past the signpost.

8 Reach the lane by the Royal Oak pub. **Turn left** up the lane to continue on our route. Towards the top of the hill, leave the lane and **turn right** on to the right-of-way track. This pleasant track gently climbs. **Keep straight ahead** at the signpost, ignoring the footpath. At the fork by several gates, **take the left fork**, following the bridleway sign. Go through the gate by the bungalow. **Turn right** on to the tarmac driveway. After the big house entrance, where the track forks, follow the bridleway marker post **straight ahead** taking the **right fork**. Ignore access to private land (garages and stables) and **keep right** on the bridleway between the fences, passing a marker post. Go through the gate.

9 Rejoin the SDW, making sure to go **left**. Go through the gate and walk on. Enjoy the scenic descent to Bramshott Bottom. From the five-way stone signpost, **go left** and up through the gate by the edge of the field to climb Harting Hill. **Watch out: slippery chalk track!** Follow the SDW back to the car park.

EXPLORE TWO SIDES OF A BEAUTIFUL DOWNLAND VALLEY

DISTANCE: 12KM/7.5MILES » **TOTAL ASCENT:** 317M/1,040FT » **START GR:** SU 879132 » **TIME:** ALLOW 3.5 HOURS
SATNAV: PO18 0HP » **MAP:** OS EXPLORER OL8, CHICHESTER, 1:25,000 » **REFRESHMENTS:** THE FOX GOES FREE, CHARLTON,
OR THE PARTRIDGE INN, SINGLETON » **NAVIGATION:** STRAIGHTFORWARD.

VIEW OVER CHARLTON FROM LEVIN DOWN

04 Explore Two Sides of a Beautiful Downland Valley

12km/7.5miles

Climb Levin Down, a biodiverse and isolated nature reserve, on a steep slope, meander down the peaceful valley, passing through the flint village of Charlton (or stopping at the pub!) before climbing up to circle Goodwood Racecourse and reach the Trundle, a viewpoint overlooking Sussex and its coastline.

Singleton » Levin Down Nature Reserve » Charlton » Goodwood Race Course » The Trundle » Singleton

Start

Singleton. Parking near the village hall or roadside. GR: SU 879132.

The Walk

Levin Down means 'leave-alone hill' and its steep slopes have enabled it to escape the plough and other human intervention. A Sussex Wildlife Trust reserve, it is a Site of Special Scientific Interest. The gorse and scrub changes with the seasons: I found it stunning in summer. There's something unexpected about life flourishing on this rugged chalk hillside: butterflies, such as green and brown hairstreaks, and chalk grassland flowers like the clustered bellflower. On the chalk heath, there's juniper, scrub warblers and finches. It's strangely isolated here given the proximity of Singleton and Charlton but the approach is steep. Keep dogs under close control because hill sheep add their own special something to the atmosphere here and are apt to appear unexpectedly.

Much of this peaceful valley has a rural 'world apart' feeling. You may see a farmer rounding up sheep and sleepy villages down below but there aren't many roads. Our route leads you through the picturesque flint houses of Charlton, passing The Fox Goes Free pub where you may wish to stop for refreshments. Alternatively, wait and call in at the Partridge in Singleton. It's a hard choice because both pubs are appealing!

Goodwood Racecourse has a huge impact on this area so this part of our route is more interesting than beautiful. Surrounding roads will be busier on a race day. Views of the valley are blocked by the course, but never mind, you are heading for the Trundle viewpoint.

From the Trundle, there are magnificent views over the estuary, Sussex countryside and the coastline. Keep your eyes open too as you walk back down into Singleton. Part of the fun of this walk is spotting Levin Down and the ubiquitous racetrack from various different vantage points on the walk. What a contrast!

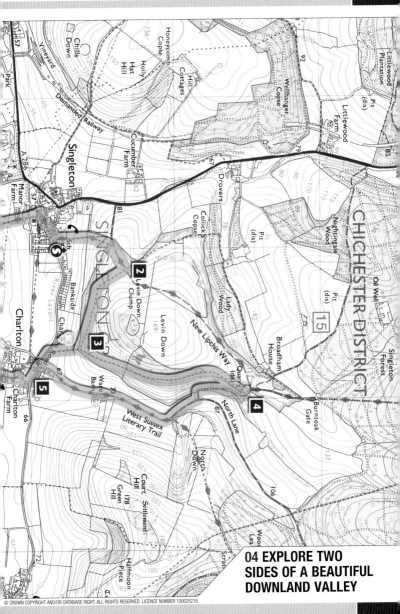

04 EXPLORE TWO SIDES OF A BEAUTIFUL DOWNLAND VALLEY

Directions – Explore Two Sides of a Beautiful Downland Valley

➤ Roughly opposite the village hall, look for the signed public footpath to the left of the bus shelter and the school. Climb **straight ahead** up the hill. At the top go through the hedge to the gate. Follow the footpath **straight ahead** to join the bridleway at the wooden waymarker signpost. **Turn right** to follow the bridleway towards the next marker post.

2 At the next marker post, **turn right** to explore Levin Down via the footpath. Go through the double gate to enter this Sussex Wildlife Trust Nature Reserve. Follow the track **straight ahead**. Go through the gate and follow the footpath as it gently leads you down and across chalk downland. Walk on along the footpath at the first gate and marker post.

3 At the gate in the corner, **don't exit** the reserve, but follow the footpath left along the fence.

⊕ **SC:** Alternatively, at the gate in the corner, **exit right** and follow the footpath down to Charlton Road, where you **turn left** to join our main route at the crossroads to head into Charlton at point 5.

Go through the next gate and follow the signed footpath **diagonally left** back up the slope. Follow the track to the next gate and continue to walk **straight ahead**. Go through a gate and leave the nature reserve. Walk straight ahead, following the track through the trees. It's indistinct but followable. Reach a gate. Go through and follow the signed footpath **right** through the field. Walk along the line of the fence to a partially obscured stile. Cross and follow the path for a short distance through the copse.

4 **Turn right** at the chalk and flint bridleway and follow it round the curve, past the entrance back into the reserve. **Turn right** at the T-junction with another bridleway. Keep straight ahead on this easy farm track towards Charlton. At the end of Downs Bridleway/North Lane, come to a crossroads.

5 At the crossroads, **turn left** into Charlton. Pass The Fox Goes Free pub. **Turn right**, passing Charlton Barns, following the lane as it curves past the phone box. **Turn left** at the wooden sign along the bridleway or lane. Pass the house and follow the bridleway **straight ahead** as signed on the marker post. The bridleway climbs the hill and is fenced on both sides. At the top, reach the racecourse and follow the bridleway **straight ahead**. Walk up the side of the racecourse. Go to the very end, past the gate across the bridleway.

6 **Turn right** at the road. Walk along the grass verge beside the flint wall of the racetrack. Follow the road along past Goodwood Country Park. Pass a playground. Pass the back of the Lennox Enclosure and then the back of the Sussex Grandstand. The road descends. Pass Horseboxes Nº 4 Car Park. At the T-junction, **turn right** for a short stretch along this road which may be busy. Pass the main racecourse entrance.

7 Just after a wooden fence, leave the tarmac to **go left** on the bridleway, following the wooden waymarker post. Follow the path through the trees past a marker post. At the gate, follow the public byway across the field. This is the Trundle! From the top of the hill, continue in the same direction, heading towards the car park. Go through the gate and follow the bridleway past the car park. You are at Seven Points Car Park.

8 **Turn right** out of the gate and on to the lane. **Double back** immediately through the wooden gate to follow the bridleway sign back round the base of the Trundle. You are heading left, initially parallel with a lane and a fence with a pylon on your right. The footpath is not clear but head diagonally across the main road and racecourse. Reach a walkers' gate by the road.

9 **Turn right** on to the road (!) for a short distance only. At the bend, **turn left** down the lane, passing the Triangle Car Park. After the junction, **head left again** on to the single track road.

10 **Go left** at the signpost and through a gate to follow the fenced footpath. Walk through the gate and continue **straight ahead** past a signpost. Follow the path back down through a gate and farm buildings and into Singleton. Follow a gate and footpath through the churchyard. **Walk left** out of the churchyard and turn right along this small residential lane. Emerge at a crossroads by the Partridge Inn. **Turn right** to return to the village hall and start point.

A WOODLAND CLIMB TO ANCIENT COMMON & HEATH

DISTANCE: 13KM/8MILES » **TOTAL ASCENT:** 311M/1,020FT » **START GR:** SU 863225 » **TIME:** ALLOW 6 HOURS **SATNAV:** GU29 0NW » **MAP:** OS EXPLORER OL33, HASLEMERE & PETERSFIELD, 1:25,000 » **REFRESHMENTS:** THE HAMILTON ARMS OR THE GLASSHOUSE CAFE, ROTHERHILL NURSERIES, STEDHAM **NAVIGATION:** LANDMARKS CAN BE LESS EVIDENT IN WOODLAND. UNMARKED TRACKS MAY MAKE OLDER HILL TRICKY. ONCE ON COMMON, USE COMPASS, BUILDINGS AND LIE OF LAND TO ORIENTATE YOURSELF BECAUSE IF UNDERGROWTH IS HIGH, LANE MAY NOT BE VISIBLE.

A 'SUNKEN' LANE

05 A Woodland Climb to Ancient Common & Heath

13km/8miles

Climb through an interesting mixture of remote and varied woodland to the lowland heathland of Woolbeding Common before returning via 'sunken' lanes and bridleways to the village of Stedham.

Stedham » Iping » Oakham Common » Titty Hill » Lambourne Copse » Older Hill » Woolbeding Common » Tote Hill » Stedham Mill » Stedham

Start

The wooden waymarker by the dead-end sign where the road forks near the church in Stedham. Roadside parking by village green or along the road towards the church. GR: SU 863225.

The Walk

If you fancy a day where you have the world all to yourself, this is a good area to head for. And what a world it is: dense and marshy woodland, ancient heathland, fairy tale cottages and unexpected, exhilarating views. Walk through a variety of woodland. In Oakham Common, fallen trees lie tangled while new life sprouts upwards. It's a great example of how woodland is constantly evolving. Birdcall provides background music whilst butterflies add colour. Step off the path and you don't just crunch the leaf litter beneath your feet, it's so deep that you sink down into it!

Near Stedham Marsh, the terrain alters. The ferns grow higher, the ground is boggier and there's water to be spotted. Buzzing insects and flickering butterflies gravitate towards the pond.

Climb up Older Hill where the trees feel forest-like on the steep slopes. It's a surprise to discover archetypal cottages, complete with log piles, on its isolated fringes. Emerge on to Woolbeding Common to discover how high you've climbed; after the dense woodland, the breeze and open views over the Weald are truly stunning. The place feels wild and remote: a feeling at odds with images that we may hold of Sussex. Eighty per cent of heathland in West Sussex has been lost over the last 200 years and so perhaps it's not surprising that we no longer naturally recognise this as 'our' landscape.

The rare lowland heathland of Woolbeding Common (SSSI) is managed by the National Trust and supports some of our rarer birds, such as the nightjar, woodlark and dartford warbler. Watch out for the 'sunken' feel of the lane near Tote Hill. These high hedges built on a stone wall flank the track on both sides to create a 'sunken' lane, a charact-eristic of Woolbeding Common where in some places, boundaries date back to medieval times.

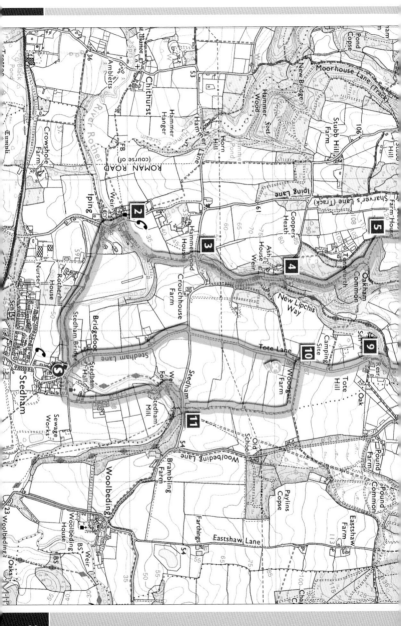

05 A WOODLAND CLIMB TO ANCIENT COMMON & HEATH

Directions – A Woodland Climb to Ancient Common & Heath

➊ Walk **straight ahead**, staying on the main lane. **Go left** at the bridleway sign before the bridge. The path runs alongside the River Rother. It climbs through a peaceful copse, then narrows alongside fields. Go through a gate on to the lane. Follow the bridleway **left** and then **straight ahead**, leaving the lane by the wooden marker at the stone gateposts. This cobbled path slopes down. At the lane, **turn right**. Cross the stone bridge.

2 At Iping Church, follow the wooden waymarker **right** across the field. The track goes through a wide gate and almost immediately **right** through a gap in the fence (horse jumps training here!). **Follow the line of the trees**, cross a stile and **continue straight ahead** across the field. Go through a gate and reach a lane.

3 Briefly **turn right** on to the lane **and then left** on to the signed mud footpath. After a climb, the path forks: **stay left**, on the same track – yet another very secluded woodland track. Keep going at the first marker post. **Turn left** on to the lane at the second marker post, passing Ash House. At the hedge, look for the wooden waymarker signpost on your left and follow the restricted byway sign straight on.

4 You are in quite dense woodland now with a 'left-alone' feel to it. At the marker post by the clearing (where ferns may be growing and you are joined by a footpath from the left), keep going. A few yards on, look for the wooden marker post where you **head left** on the footpath. This path cuts through ferns and climbs.

5 At the top, follow the bridleway **right**. Go through the gate and walk straight ahead across the edge of the field. Go through the next gate and follow the bridleway **straight ahead**. At the T-junction of paths, near Stedham Marsh, **go left** on the public right of way so that you keep going in the same direction. Before the house on Titty Hill, take the byway going **right**. Stay on it. You are walking through marshy woodland. Pass a small pond on your left. The path becomes more open and the byway becomes Lambourne Lane.

6 At the marker post, **walk right** along the wide, concrete track. Walk through Slathurst Farm and follow the track **right**. At the wooden marker post, by the fork, **go straight ahead**. The path bends left. Keep following the track through the fields.

7 At the road, **turn right and then left** on to the footpath diagonally opposite. Cross the stile and walk across the rough field to the stile in the top right corner. Follow the footpath as it climbs up into the woods. At the three-way marker post, **keep straight ahead** through Older Hill Copse. The path narrows and climbs. Towards the top, there's another three-way marker post, this time surrounded by large stones. **Go right** here on the track. After a while, the path runs alongside a fence. There's a red-roofed house and views open up to your right. Follow the marker post **straight ahead** as the path wends its way through the wood. **Turn left** at the signpost by Barnetts Cottage. Follow the narrow track as it wends its way up across Woolbeding Common until you reach the lane.

8 **Turn right** on to this very quiet lane. Pass the National Trust access road on your left. **Turn right** after around 900m where the footpath crosses the road: as you turn to leave the road, **bear left**. Briefly head back across the common and soon reach a road. **Cross** the road and follow the footpath to the left of the National Trust *Woolbeding* sign. Keep walking **straight ahead** on the bridleway at the four-way marker post. At the next marker post, **keep left** to go on the drive passing beside Ivy Cottage. Follow the path round and where it forks left, **keep straight ahead**, passing in front of the red-tiled house. Ignore the next bridleway leading right and instead **keep straight ahead** on this tarmac byway.

9 The bridleway turns into a lane. **Walk straight ahead**, ignoring the footpath sign going to the left by the house. The lane has a distinctive 'sunken' feel with high banks where hedges have been built on stone walls on both sides. Pass the footpath on the right to Stedham Campsite.

> **SC**: Keep straight ahead on the lane to return directly to Stedham and parking. Recommended in bad weather as the main route crosses a ford.

10 **Follow the footpath left** just past the barn at Woodgate Farm, heading along the left side of the hedge. As the red roof of the house ahead comes into view, look for an overgrown and **easy-to-miss stile on your right** beside a telephone pole. **Turn right** across the stile. Follow the footpath across the fields with beautiful open views. Cross another stile and continue. Cross a third stile and reach the lane.

11 **Turn right** on to the lane for a short distance. Soon, **turn left** on to the footpath. The path emerges by the weir and ford. Cross the narrow bridge to Stedham Mill. **Walk right** along the lane back into Stedham, passing the churchyard and church.

BLACK DOWN, UP HIGH & INSPIRING

DISTANCE: 10.5KM/6.5MILES » **TOTAL ASCENT:** 377M/1,237FT » **START GR:** SU 935271 » **TIME:** ALLOW 4 HOURS
SATNAV: GU28 9ET » **MAP:** OS EXPLORER OL33, HASLEMERE & PETERSFIELD, 1:25,000 » **REFRESHMENTS:** THE NOAH'S ARK,
LURGASHALL » **NAVIGATION:** THE OPTIONAL ROUTE BACK ACROSS BLACK DOWN FOLLOWS A LARGELY UNSIGNED NATIONAL
TRUST TRAIL. IT'S SIGNED AT THE START AND EVENTUALLY MEETS A BRIDLEWAY BY SOME STEPS.

ORIENTATION POINT AT TEMPLE OF THE WINDS

06 Black Down, Up High & Inspiring: 10.5km/6.5miles
Tennyson's Summer Home

Climb gradually through farmland and ancient woods to Black Down's viewpoint, 'Temple of the Winds', meander on the plateau through broadleaf woods and sandy pine forests, descending via Tennyson's Lane and his summer home, Aldworth, before returning across fields.

Lurgashall » Windfallwood Common » Blackdown Farm » Black Down » Temple of the Winds » Tennyson's Lane / Aldworth House / Quellwood Common » Spring Coppice » Lurgashall

Start

White signpost on Lurgashall village green. Roadside parking. GR: SU 935271.

The Walk

Black Down forms part of the North Weald Greensand Ridge and, at 280 metres, it is the highest point in the county of Sussex and the South Downs National Park. Our starting point is Lurgashall, the quintessential English village. Eat at the picturesque pub overlooking the green or, if you prefer, Black Down offers several absorbing viewpoints with handy benches well placed for picnics.

Walk through grazing fields, orchards and Spring Coppice, a 'left-alone' wood with abundant foxgloves. After a short section on Jobson's Lane, enjoy a quieter stretch through Quellwood Common, once ancient wood pasture. As you climb towards and beyond Blackdown Farm, you are rewarded by an increasingly stunning series of views over Windfall Wood, hazy fields and distant downland.

Onwards through steep National Trust woodland where a moss-covered tree makes a good place to pause. Once on the plateau, our route meanders. Rest at a bench to admire the view or use the orientation point at the Temple of the Winds to locate yourself with reference to distant Sussex locations. The bulk of Black Down is covered in pine woodland. There are sandy paths scattered with pinecones and trees anchored in steep slopes. In places, the landscape opens up, where pine and birch scrub is currently being restored to heathland to benefit wildlife.

Black Down is best known as the site of Tennyson's summer home, Aldworth. The poet was known to take long walks over Black Down and Tennyson's Lane, with its sunken appearance, is named in his honour.

Tennyson's study faced south over the Weald and inspired him to write this poem:

*You came, and looked and loved the view
Long-known and loved by me,
Green Sussex fading into blue
With one gray glimpse of sea.*

COMMON FOXGLOVE, DIGITALIS PURPUREA

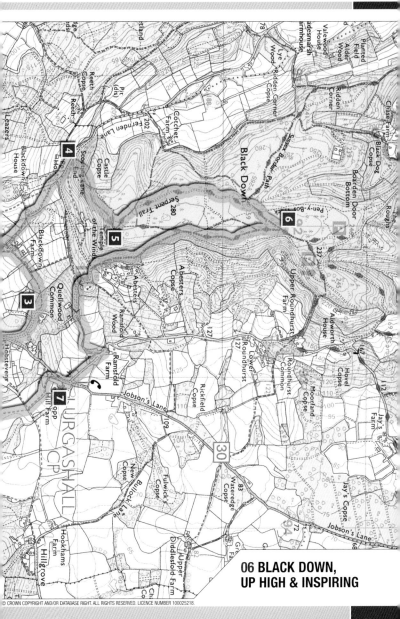

**06 BLACK DOWN,
UP HIGH & INSPIRING**

Directions – Black Down, Up High & Inspiring

➐ From the white signpost, walk along the lane in the direction of Haslemere. At the end of the green, cross the lane to take the signposted footpath. Go through the kissing gate and follow the line of the fence through the orchard. Go **straight ahead**, crossing a series of kissing gates in quick succession. Follow path through Spring Coppice and on through more fields.

2 At the end of the wood, where path joins with bridleway, you must instead cross the stile to follow the footpath across the field, following the line of the fence. At the copse where three fields join, walk **left** and pass a footpath signpost. At the next stile, walk about 10m and **turn right** at the signpost to walk across the field towards the house. Go through the gate and walk **left** staying on the footpath as signed on the waymarker post. Walk **right** in front of the garage and then **left** to exit Hobstevens Farm. At Jobson's Lane, **walk right** for 25m then **turn left** along the quieter Quell Lane which runs through mature woodland.

3 **Walk left** into woodland at the wooden waymarker about 30 metres after the five-bar gate. Climb up, passing the pig pens, following the track **straight ahead**. Walk past a row of cottages. Where the stony track forks, walk **right** up the hill. Pass through the gated entrance to Blackdown Farm. Continue on the tarmac lane climbing right. At the top, climb through the stone stile, exiting Blackdown Park. Continue **straight ahead**.

4 At the gap, walk **right**. Follow the bridleway to the right of the National Trust (NT) sign, making a steep but shady climb up through the woods. Go through a gate and walk on up. Follow the meandering path until you reach a three-way bridleway marker post. Take the path on the **left**. Come to a three-way bridleway marker post. Go **right** to the 'Temple of the Winds,' a stone seat and orientation point.

5 Return to the three-way bridleway marker post, go **straight ahead**, noting the Serpent Trail emblem. Follow it through the woods and bear **right**, heading downwards. Join with a path bordering heathland and enjoy magnificent views and a topography point. At the signpost, head **right**, towards Tennyson's Lane car park. This path soon forks again: walk **right**, still staying on the Serpent Trail. You feel like you're doubling back through the pine trees.

6 Reach a three-way signpost and turn right. Take the **left fork** at the next signpost and continue down. The track is rough, unmarked and snakes along the top of steep-sloped woodland. Ignore offshoots and eventually the track broadens into a wider mud path with a steep slope to your left and the ground rising above to your right. Walk straight on past a signpost. Pass some wooden steps. At the signpost, take the **left fork**, heading down the hill. Go through the gate and stay on the bridleway. It runs alongside a fence for a while. Emerge at the end of Fernden Lane with a NT sign to your right. Walk **straight ahead** down leafy Quell Lane. Ignore the first footpath and the next restricted byway on your right. **Turn left** along an easy-to-miss bridleway opposite Quellhurst. This path can be overgrown with nettles. At the end of the bridleway **turn right** for a short distance along the lane.

7 At the T-junction, **turn right** towards Lurgashall. Almost immediately, follow the footpath signed on the wooden waymarker which initially runs parallel with the road. Cross the stile and walk straight across the field. At the far side, a footpath crosses your path. Go **straight ahead** over the stile. Walk **diagonally right** across the field to the far side. Go through the metal gate and see a yellow arrow on a marker post. Walk **straight ahead** to follow the edge of trees down the right-hand side of the field. Cross a stile by a wooden waymarked gate. **Turn right** and let this nice and easy track lead you back to Lurgashall. Emerge at the pub by the village green.

ANCIENT EBERNOE COMMON & MILK WOOD

DISTANCE: 10.4KM/6.5MILES » **TOTAL ASCENT:** 160M/525FT » **START GR:** SU 951294 » **TIME:** ALLOW 5 HOURS
SATNAV: GU28 9HP » **MAP:** OS EXPLORER OL33, HASLEMERE & PETERSFIELD, 1:25,000 » **REFRESHMENTS:** HALF MOON INN,
NORTHCHAPEL, OR STAG INN, BALLS CROSS » **NAVIGATION:** STRAIGHTFORWARD. BEST TO STICK TO THE MAIN PATHS AT
EBERNOE COMMON.

07 Ancient Ebernoe Common & Milk Wood

10.4km/6.5miles

An easy walk exploring woods of varying character and ancient common including a section of Sussex Wildlife Trust's Ebernoe Common Nature Reserve with an optional link to a welcoming pub at Balls Cross.

Northchapel » Burrell's Wood » Colhook Common » Ebernoe Common » Butcherlands Nature Reserve (OR) » Balls Cross (OR) » Ebernoe Common » Wet Wood » Northchapel

Start

Half Moon Inn in Northchapel. Park roadside or lay-bys on or near the A283 by the village green and school in Northchapel. Alternatively, past the school, the village hall has a large car park. GR: SU 951294.

The Walk

Ebernoe Common and Butcherlands Reserve are well worth the walk from Northchapel. As well as being historically and environmentally interesting, this easy, flat walk runs through one of the core forest areas of the West Weald. It's also off the beaten track and with a mid-point pub. Take the optional route past Butcherlands Nature Reserve to the friendly, seventeenth century Stag Inn at Balls Cross where you will find stone floors, open fires, Hall and Woodhouse ale and a large back garden backing on to woodland.

Our trail follows the main path through the reserve. The high forest and open grassland are significant habitats with glades, droveways and shallow ponds all playing their part. This rich 'mosaic of interconnected habitats' is enabling a number of species to flourish including lichens, fungi, 37 species of butterfly, and bats such as the rare barbastelle bat and Bechstein's bat. The birds that breed here are too numerous to list but include sparrowhawks, buzzards, tawny owls, barn owls and various woodpeckers. Sussex Wildife Trust is hoping to use grazing to diversify the structure of this woodland and to create and maintain open glades. As you walk through Ebernoe, look at the contrasts: young and veteran trees, 'understorey' and canopy, beech and oak, dense and sparse, open and closed.

Ebernoe Common is thought to have originated as an area of woodland used to fatten pigs whilst Butcherland was part of a medieval field system. This area could be described as a 'cultural landscape' developed from a medieval pattern of fields, hedges and woods, which have evolved over centuries of interaction between people and nature. It's possible today to walk through Ebernoe and wonder just how the natural forest of lowland England might have once looked.

HOLY TRINITY CHURCH AT EBERNOE

**07 ANCIENT EBERNOE
COMMON & MILK WOOD**

Directions – Ancient Ebernoe Common & Milk Wood

➏ Take the public footpath opposite the Half Moon Inn on the A283. Soon, pass the church and **walk straight ahead** through the graveyard. Follow the grassy path straight ahead. It runs along the top of the field and through a gap in the hedge. Cross the stile to the road.

2 **Turn right** to follow the public bridleway down to the right of the stone farmhouse. Where the track forks by a gate, **follow the bridleway left** through the woods. At the crossroads with another bridleway, **keep straight ahead** through the woods.

3 Cross the tarmac farm track and **walk straight ahead**. This narrow bridleway may initially be brambly but soon improves.

> **SC: Turn left** along the farm track to join up with main route at point 7.

Walk straight ahead, staying on this bridleway, crossing the grassy track to the gate. Keep following the signed bridleway through the woods. Emerge on to a stony track. **Turn right** and **briefly right again** to see a wooden waymarker. There are several handy benches near this pond/green. **Turn left** off the road to follow the public bridleway by taking the left-hand fork. Pass a balloon launching field (portaloos!). Stay on the bridleway. **Keep right** at the campsite, staying on the stony bridleway.

4 At the 'lane' junction, **follow the signed tarmac footpath left**. Walk past the large pond on Colhook Common. The path continues on through Blackwool Farm Trout Fishery. Follow the public footpath sign **straight ahead** out of the car park. Keep walking for some time, passing two footpaths leading left. The path leads you on to the edge of Ebernoe Common.

5 When you reach a three-way footpath sign, you have a choice:

> **OR** **Turn right at the path** to walk past Butcherlands Nature Reserve and on to the Stag Inn at Balls Cross. **Ignore** the signed public footpath on your right. On your left, notice the Sussex Wildlife Trust entrance to Butcherland Fields. It's well worth a gander. Stay on this public footpath passing Sparkes Farm. At the lane, **turn right**. Reach Balls Cross and turn right briefly for the Stag Inn.

For the main route, go left to walk through Ebernoe Common Nature Reserve. Stay on this wide mud track for a short distance only. **Walk left** following the wooden waymarker as the footpath leaves the wide mud track. Head through a gate. You are now in Sussex Wildlife Trust's Ebernoe Common Nature Reserve. Continue on this track through a mixture of woodland and small glades. The end of the footpath is marked by three posts as you reach another footpath. **Turn right** at the end of the track by the footpath sign. **Turn left** to go through the gate and leave Ebernoe Common along the driveway. Pass by the distinctive red brick Holy Trinity Church at Ebernoe (worth a look). Walk straight ahead on the white arrowed public footpath (driveway).

6 Turn left at the road and almost immediately and before the phone box, **turn right**. Follow the footpath signs. When you reach the three-way sign after Ebernoe House, **go straight ahead** down the slope. Cross the 'bridge' and the stile to emerge on to an open field. Go **straight ahead** and then **turn right** at the far side of the field to exit the field via a stile in the far right corner. **Walk straight ahead** down the side of the crop field.

7 Cross the tarmac footpath and climb over the stile to follow the footpath **straight ahead**. Cross the next stile and **head right**, following the sign, taking the footpath along the line of hedge. See the Air Navigational Radio Beacon on your right. Cross right into the next field to **follow the footpath sign left** continuing in the same direction as you have been walking. A short way into the pine woods, **follow a footpath sign right**.

8 Reach the four-way junction and **walk straight ahead** staying on the footpath. Follow the signed path into the woods. Soon, **turn right** and **rejoin the bridleway from the start of your walk**. Walk past the stone farmhouse. **Either** return by the footpath that you used earlier **or turn left along the road** to reach Northchapel School and green.

RIVER ARUN & EASY DOWNLAND LOOP

DISTANCE: 14KM/8.7MILES » **TOTAL ASCENT:** 142M/466FT » **START GR:** TQ 020070 » **TIME:** ALLOW 4-5 HOURS
SATNAV: BN18 9JG » **MAP:** OS EXPLORER OL10, ARUNDEL & PULBOROUGH, 1:25,000 » **REFRESHMENTS:** THE BLACK
RABBIT, OFFHAM, OR THE GEORGE AT BURPHAM **NAVIGATION:** BURPHAM - THE ROADS ARE DIFFERENT FROM HOW YOU'D
EXPECT IT TO LOOK FROM THE MAP BUT SHOULD BE STRAIGHTFORWARD IF YOU FOLLOW OUR DIRECTIONS.

RIVER ARUN AND ARUNDEL CASTLE

08 River Arun & Easy Downland Loop

14km/8.7miles

An easy meander from Arundel Castle along the riverbanks of the Arun diverting to the country pub in Burpham before returning with a small downland loop.

Arundel » Offham » South Stoke » Burpham » Warningcamp Hill » Warningcamp » Arundel

Start

Mill Road car park, opposite Arundel Castle, or roadside parking along Mill Road. GR: TQ 020070.

The Walk

One thousand year old Arundel Castle may often be seen as you follow this route, standing sentry over the river and impressing us with the simple lines of its rising towers against the sky. It is still a significant point of reference today and gives us a good idea of just how such these buildings must have dominated the landscape in years gone by.

This route follows the banks of the River Arun making for some easy walking. There's something about water that is very contemplative and relaxing and this river won't disappoint. However, for those who hanker after change, there's an optional route provided which climbs away from the river on a bridleway between Offham and South Stoke. This stretch is rougher and the paths may be overgrown but it provides some variety. Whichever way you choose to go,

the land between Offham and South Stoke takes on a more remote feel than the area beside Arundel. The hamlet of South Stoke, with its small church spire and flint walls, is picturesque and a good place to cross the river. There's more of a woodland feel to the paths on the east side of the river.

Given its location, it's no surprise that there has been a pub at Burpham for over 300 years! The George at Burpham continues to provide a warm welcome to villagers and visitors, although it is perhaps more gastro-pub than spit and sawdust. A car park near the pub makes a good alternative start to this walk. A steep climb takes you out of Burpham but the bridleway is hard-surfaced and, from the top, views expand towards the sea and Arundel castle. Enjoy the shady descent past poppy-strewn fields.

Return to the river banks through the low downland and woodland of Angmering Park Estate where open glades of long grass give a feeling of wildness, reinforced by a grasshopper chorus.

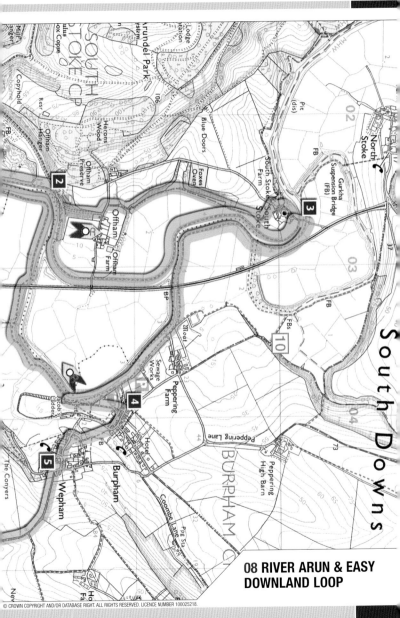

08 RIVER ARUN & EASY DOWNLAND LOOP

Directions – River Arun & Easy Downland Loop

➌ From the far side of Mill Road car park, follow the footpath to the right which runs along the river bank. The castle sits on the hill to your left, the River Arun is to your right. Pass the Environment Agency sluice gate. The path runs alongside the Wildfowl Reserve.

2 Come to the Black Rabbit at Offham.

> **OR** Join the lane, so that you pass the Black Rabbit pub. Walk up the short hill. At the T-junction, **turn left** towards South Stoke. Almost immediately, look for the bridleway which is just after the lay-by. **Turn right** on to the bridleway, passing through the wooden gate. Walk downhill on this narrow winding track. Pass Fox Cottage. Walk beside the stream/ditch. Go through the gate. Walk on, following the course of the stream. Pass by a wooden fence. Keep going along this track, with the bulrushes parallel but not right next to you. Follow the track round and up, emerging opposite South Stokes Farm.

To stay on our river bank route, walk **straight ahead** through the car park. Follow the wooden waymarked footpath into the trees. Go over the stile and back on to the river bank. Ignore the first bridge and continue **straight ahead** across the stiles. Walk towards the small church spire, soon passing South Stoke.

3 **Turn right** at South Stoke Bridge. Cross the river and **immediately turn right** again to join the footpath on the river bank. Cross a stile and walk on. At the second stile, keep straight ahead. Walk on. Go across the railway crossing and over the stile. Follow the grassy track as it curves right. A few steps after the signpost, **turn right** to cross a stile. Walk across the clearing and through a gate. Follow the footpath as it narrows and climbs between the trees.

Go right at the signpost, sometimes glimpsing the river to your right. Follow the public footpath to its end.

By the stile and signpost, **turn left** to climb up the steps, following the public footpath. At the top, **walk along the fenced track** and through a gate, passing a children's play area on your left. Continue **straight ahead** through the recreation ground. Pass the timber pavilion and reach The George at Burpham.

> It is possible to return to Arundel via the river bank path. Retrace your steps to the river bank and cross the stile at the base of the steps. You may either follow the footpath along the river bank or take the footpath which runs almost parallel with the railway line, straight across the fields. The distance is similar but it's flatter. Rejoin main route at point 7.

4 Turn right out of the pub and down the lane. **Turn down the first lane on the right**. Cross the stile and walk across the field to the steps. At the top of the steps, **go right** keeping the fence on your right side. Head for the stile. Walk between the two fences. Cross the next stile and descend the steep steps to the road. **Turn left** and walk up the lane to a T-junction. **Turn right** on to the road.

5 Almost immediately, **turn left** up the bridleway. This is a steep climb out of Burpham. At the top of the hill, leave the tarmac to **walk right on the signed bridleway**. Descend on the chalk and flint path. You are now entering Angmering Estate. At the wooden waymarker, where the path forks, **turn right**. Soon, at the next wooden waymarker, follow the Monarch's Way bridleway **right** through the gate. Stay on the bridleway as you pass two signs, heading for the woods. At the third wooden waymarker, **go right** along the track beside the trees. Go through the gate and follow the path through the woods.

6 Turn left at the road, following Monarch's Way. At Warningcamp crossroads, **turn right** towards the youth hostel. Keep straight ahead at the railway crossing.

7 Head left towards the castle. Go through the gate to follow the public footpath along the riverbank back to Arundel. Go over the stile, past the private boat moorings. At the very end, **turn left**. Go through the white gateposts along the pub footpath to Arundel High Street. Go across the bridge and **turn right** into Mill Road.

AN INVIGORATING HIKE TO THE LEE SIDE OF THE DOWNS

DISTANCE: 18KM/11MILES » **TOTAL ASCENT:** 376M/1,233FT » **START GR:** TQ 001109 » **TIME:** ALLOW 5 HOURS
SATNAV: BN18 9FD » **MAP:** OS EXPLORER OL10, ARUNDEL & PULBOROUGH, 1:25,000 » **REFRESHMENTS:** WHITEWAYS
CAFE, WHITEWAYS CAR PARK; THE WHITE HORSE, SUTTON; TEAROOM AT BIGNOR ROMAN VILLA (OPEN MARCH UNTIL OCTOBER);
THE SQUIRE AND HORSE, BURY; SEVERAL TEAROOMS AND RESTAURANTS AT HOUGHTON BRIDGE AND AMBERLEY
NAVIGATION: STRAIGHTFORWARD. THE USE OF THE QUIET LANE BETWEEN WEST BURTON AND BURY IS TO AVOID POORLY-
MAINTAINED AND SIGNED FOOTPATHS IN THIS AREA.

Enjoy the South Downs Way before detouring to a secluded pub and returning home past Bignor Roman Villa, an English vineyard, a literary death-place and along the banks of the River Arun to Amberley tearooms and Amberley Station.

Whiteways Car Park » Bury Hill » Westburton Hill » Bignor » Sutton » Bignor » Grevatt Wood » West Burton » Bury » Houghton Bridge, Amberley » Bury Hill » Whiteways Car Park

Start

Whiteways car park off roundabout junction of A284/A29/B2139. Can also be started from Amberley Station, but be aware that the museum car park (next to the station) will be locked when the last visitor leaves! GR: TQ 001109.

The Walk

This is a rewarding stretch of the South Downs Way. Cross the A29 and you notice an immediate change in the landscape: trees! The woodland adds colour and texture to the downland. Skirt round Bignor Hill and divert to Sutton, following the footpaths beside an archetypal babbling brook. The White Horse is a relaxing country pub with a traditional yet modern atmosphere.

Stop to explore Bignor Roman Villa, with its well-known mosaic floors, and discover why this downland location was selected for such a significant settlement. Walk on through Nyetimber, the largest vineyard in the UK. They specialise in premium sparkling wine as the chalk and greensand soil here is well suited to its production. Walk well-trodden tracks close to the old Roman road and pass by Grevatt Wood, where we saw deer grazing. Follow the lane for some straightforward walking, and pass an interesting mix of historic houses and enjoy views up to the Downs.

Bury is an attractive flint village. Walk past Bury House, the home of John Galsworthy – the playwright and author best known for the Forsyte Saga novels and the winner of the Nobel Prize for Literature in 1932. It was reputedly on seeing the Downs, before he had even set foot inside Bury House, that he decided he had to have the property, declaring, 'This is the place'.

By the river, see Bury Wharf. The ferry no longer runs, but for years it was an integral part of village life. Head for Houghton Bridge where there's a choice of riverside eating places, and Amberley Station. The pleasant links to Whiteways car park, the pub at Sutton and Houghton Bridge are each about a mile long and can be avoided if preferred.

09 AN INVIGORATING HIKE TO THE LEE SIDE OF THE DOWNS

Directions – An Invigorating Hike to the Lee Side of the Downs

➌ Follow the bridleway sign by the middle of the car park into Houghton Forest. At the bridleway marker post next to the big tree, **turn right**. Emerge at another marker post and **turn left**. At the next marker post, **follow the bridleway right**. Walk on for some way until you hit the SDW at the signed junction.

2 Turn left to join the SDW. Stay on this chalk track for a considerable time.

3 Pass a large triple barn and come to a four-way wooden waymarker at Westburton Hill. Take care here. You must leave the SDW, which veers left, and instead **walk straight ahead** up the slope on the bridleway.

> **◐ SC**: A bridleway goes right to West Burton. **Turn right** at the lane, and rejoin the main route on the West Burton Road in point 6. Shortens main route by 3.5 miles.

Staying on the main route, look out for the steep wooded escarpment dropping away on the right. At the unsigned crossroads, **keep straight ahead** on the same track. **Descend the hill** on the chalk and flint track through the woods. **Walk right** at the tarmac lane, following it down the hill to Bignor. Walk through Jay's Farm.

4 **Turn left** along the lane immediately after the farmhouse, walking past the out-building (To avoid the link to Sutton **turn right** to find white signpost: see below). After the bend, ignore the first waymarked footpath, which goes left, and **stay on the lane**. Just before the red house, Charmans, **turn left down the second footpath**. The track runs alongside a stream with a weir. Cross a couple of footbridges, pass a red brick house. **Turn left** over another footbridge, cross a stile and **walk straight ahead** across the field. At the top of the hill, continue across a stile or through a gap to **walk straight ahead** across the next field. Go through a gap in the hedge by the waymarker post and walk along the track. Emerge by The White Horse in Sutton. Return via the same footpaths to the West Sussex County Council signpost just beyond Jay Farm. At the white signpost, **turn left** to follow the lane into Bignor (signed for Sutton, which could be confusing).

5 **Walk right** on the first public footpath along the dead-end lane. Follow the footpath through Nyetimber Vineyard. Cross the drive to Bignor Roman Villa. The path continues alongside the vineyard. **Turn left** by the end of the field by the marker post to follow

the path as it diverts around Hadworth House. **Follow the signposts right and right again** until you are walking along the line of the hedge and fence. Go through the gate in the deer fence. Follow the bridleway left. At the end of the field, follow the path into the woods, immediately **turning right** at the wooden sign to follow the bridleway.

6 **Turn right** at the lane. Stay on this lane for some time, passing a road junction with turn-offs to Bignor and Sutton. Continue round the bend **towards Bury**. Stay on the lane. **Keep straight ahead** past Cokes farm. **Follow the road as it curves left** towards Bury. Pass Burton Manor and Bury School, where a pavement starts.

7 At the A29, **turn right** and **cross the road to turn immediately left** into Bury village. Walk along the pavement, following the lane. Pass Bury House. Continue on **straight ahead** past the school and the church. Reach Bury Wharf by the River Arun. **Turn right** to follow the footpath along the bank. Climb over a couple of stiles and through a couple of gates.

8 At the next path junction you have a choice:

> To divert to Houghton Bridge or Amberley continue straight ahead **along the riverbank** until you reach a footbridge. **Cross the river** and **turn right** to follow the footpath along the river bank to Houghton Bridge. (For Amberley Station, turn left up the B2139.)
>
> To reach the main route from Amberley (if travelling by train) or to return to point 8 from Houghton Bridge, go along the footpath between the railway bridge and Houghton Bridge. Cross the stile and walk **straight ahead**. Bear left before the fence. Walk alongside the river. Cross the stile and continue along the riverbank. **Turn left** across the footbridge. **Turn right** along the SDW, signed to *Littleton Farm*. **Turn left** at point 8, still following the SDW.

For the main route: **from point 8 follow the SDW away from the river**; go through a gate. Go round a corner then **turn left** through another gate. Soon reach a minor road crossing and continue straight ahead on the SDW. Climb the chalk path up the hill. Cross the A29 and **turn right then left** away from the road, following the SDW signs. At the junction (point 2), **turn left** leaving the SDW to return to the start. For those starting at Amberley Station, go straight ahead to follow main route on the SDW from point 2.

HISTORIC ARUN FLOODPLAIN

DISTANCE: 22KM/13.7MILES (OR TWO SHORTER LOOPS) » **TOTAL ASCENT:** 360M/1,181FT (235M/771FT AMBERLEY LOOP ONLY) » **START GR:** PULBOROUGH STATION TQ 042186; COLDWALTHAM TQ 030162; STOPHAM BRIDGE TQ032183 » **TIME:** 8-9 HOURS DEPENDING ON STOPS; 5.5 HOURS FOR AMBERLEY OR PULBOROUGH LOOP » **SATNAV:** PULBOROUGH STATION RH20 1DP; COLDWALTHAM RH20 1QA; STOPHAM BRIDGE RH20 1DS » **MAP:** OS EXPLORER OL10, ARUNDEL & PULBOROUGH, 1:25,000 » **REFRESHMENTS:** THE WHITE HART, STOPHAM BRIDGE; THE LABOURING MAN, COLDWALTHAM; THE BLACK HORSE AND AMBERLEY VILLAGE TEAROOM (OPENING TIMES VARY), AMBERLEY; THE SPORTSMAN, CROSS GATE; CAFE AT RSPB, PULBOROUGH BROOKS; CHEQUERS HOTEL, PULBOROUGH » **NAVIGATION:** PATH NOT OBVIOUS ON ENTRANCE TO AMBERLEY WILD BROOKS AT GATE.

OLD STOPHAM BRIDGE

10 Historic Arun Floodplain

Pass ancient monuments on historic tracks, follow the abandoned canal, meander through spectacular Amberley Wild Brooks and Pulborough Brooks Nature Reserves, climb Amberley Mount, choosing from shortcut and refreshment options to tailor this big walk to your needs.

Pulborough » Stopham Bridge » Hardham Priory » Coldwaltham » Amberley Wild Brooks » Amberley » Amberley Mount » Rackham » Greatham » Wiggonholt » Pulborough Brooks » Pulborough

Start
Pulborough Station. Car park busy in the week (parking charge). GR: TQ 042186.

Alternatives Starts
Roadside parking on Brook Lane (please park considerately without blocking gateways). Cross bridge, joining walk at point 7. GR: TQ 030162. Free car park at Stopham Bridge, opposite garden centre. Join walk at point 3. GR: TQ 032183.

The Walk
Amberley Wild Brooks is arresting. Something about these wide-open grazing fields and untamed marshes buffered by the Downs draws you there and makes you want to stay. Rightly 'owned' by the wildlife that it supports, this significant nature reserve (SWT/RSPB) is renowned for attracting wildfowl, such as Bewick's swans, and is highly important for plant life. Feeder ditches from chalk springs and peat-filtered underground water create raised bogs. Such complex hydrology enables over half of British aquatic plant species to exist here in a spectacular underwater forest, which in turn supports many rare insects, including dragonflies.

The climb to Amberley Mount provides a good contrast, enabling you to enjoy the Arun floodplain from above. Look out for butterflies such as the Duke of Burgundy near SSSI Springhead Estate, one of only a handful of downland sites where this severely threatened species is regularly recorded. Enjoy too, vistas south towards the sea.

Walking the Arun floodplain is like a trek through time. Our trail encounters a Norman motte and bailey site, a Roman causeway and remains, a dismantled railway track, an abandoned canal and two ancient monuments, old Stopham Bridge and Hardham Priory, possibly the oldest house in Sussex. Refreshments include the riverside White Hart at Stopham Bridge, the welcoming Labouring Man at Coldwaltham, the Black Horse and Sportsman pubs, Amberley Village Tearoom and the cafe at RSPB Pulborough Brooks.

Our trail leads you through a second, highly renowned RSPB reserve, Pulborough Brooks. After climbing through rare heathland, drop in at the Visitor Centre or stop at a hide. There are several places on this walk which warrant time spent exploring so I've provided shortcut and parking options.

10 HISTORIC ARUN FLOODPLAIN

Directions – Historic Arun Floodplain

➊ Opposite the station, pick up the signed public footpath next to the bike shelter. It runs alongside the railway line. At the end, **turn left** over the railway bridge and walk along Coombelands Lane. Ignore the footpath going right.

2 **Turn left** along the wooden waymarked footpath beside the five-bar gate. Follow this muddy track towards the trees. Pass the anti-artillery pillbox and keep going. Reach the driveway by the house and follow the bridleway **straight ahead** as signed on the marker post. You are walking through Pulborough Park Plantation. Walk past the gate and **turn left** along the bridleway. (Note: there's a motte and bailey site just up in the trees here on Park Mound.) Follow the well-defined path. At the marker post follow the bridleway as it curves **left**. The path runs along the edge of the trees on a low ridge. At the next marker post, go **straight ahead** on the bridleway. Descend to the road and cross over.

3 This is the White Hart pub at Stopham Bridge. **Walk left** past the pub and along the old road. Go through the car park. Note garden centre opposite with facilities.

4 Follow the public footpath **right** through the kissing gate. **Walk diagonally left** along this mud track which is the Wey-South path. Cross the footbridge and follow the signed footpath diagonally left. Use the small wooden footbridge. Head for the wooden kissing gate. Go through and follow the footpath sign across the bridge. Walk past the water treatment works. Go through the gate which is across the road. **Turn right** along a signed public footpath. **Turn left** along a mud track before the office-type ware-house building. You are still on the Wey-South Path. Go through the gate and **turn right**. You are walking along the dismantled railway line, which is now a farm track. (Divert **straight ahead** through the gate to see the Roman remains where Staine Street (a Roman road and now a track) crosses the dismantled railway track.)

To continue on the main route, turn left at footpath sign. Go through metal gate and across the field. Head to the left of trees and across the footbridge. Go through gate and cross the A29.

5 **Turn left**, away from road to follow a public footpath across the stile. Glimpse Hardham Priory off to your **diagonal left**. It's an ancient monument and possibly the oldest house in Sussex. Cross the stile ahead to follow the public footpath down into the copse. This narrow uneven mud track runs alongside the abandoned canal in a line of trees.

6 Reach the lane and **turn left**. This next stretch is on a busier than ideal road. It's a necessary evil if you wish to link Coldwaltham with Wigginholt.

> **OR** **to The Labouring Man pub in Coldwaltham: Turn right** along lane. Soon **turn right again** following a signed public footpath across a stile. At the end of the field, **cross the stile and walk straight ahead**. Cross a pedestrian railway crossing and **follow path left**. Emerge on residential road and follow it round. **Turn right** along road at small T-junction and follow signed footpath **right** between two fences. At Southern Water gates, **go left** along narrow track. At A29, **turn right** then **right again** along Old London Road to the pub!

Back on the main route, pass Waltham Brooks car park and cross Greatham Bridge.

7 For Amberley Wild Brooks and the South Downs Way (SDW), **turn right**, climbing over the stile to follow the public footpath along the river bank.

> **SC**: To go straight to Pulborough Brooks, continue walking along the lane in the direction of Storrington. Reach T-junction midway through point 15 on the main route.

Cross the next stile and **walk straight ahead** on the narrow track. Emerge on to a wide mud and shingle track. **Turn right** following the wooden waymarker. Pass a lime kiln and follow the track as it curves left at a signpost and on through Glebe and Quell farm buildings. **Turn right** at the wooden sign, following the public footpath as it branches off. Go through the five-bar gate and **turn sharp left** to follow signed public footpath.

DIRECTIONS CONTINUE OVERLEAF ▶

Directions — Historic Arun Floodplain continued...

8 Go through the gate and **walk right**, along the edge of the field. Track not obvious. You are following the Wey-South Path through RSPB land. **Walk straight ahead** across the footbridge at the 'Dangerous Marsh' and wooden waymarker signs. Cross the second footbridge and follow the grassy track through Amberley Wild Brooks. Go over the stile (or through the gate). Follow the track right at the wooden waymarker by the next gate. (Path may be muddy and slippery!) Go through the kissing gate and climb the small slope.

9 At the top of the hill, **go left**. You are in Amberley.

> ☞ **SC**: To save 2 miles and avoid downland stretch, keep **straight ahead** along the lane, heading towards Cross Gate. Pass a pub at Cross Gate and re-join the main route at point 14.

To climb to Amberley Mount and see a short but beautiful stretch of the SDW, **turn right**, passing the Black Horse pub. Walk down through the village, passing Amberley Village Tea Room. Pass a school, keeping straight ahead. Cross Turnpike Road and walk straight ahead, climbing steeply up Mill Lane.

10 At the top, **go left**, along this tarmac byway section of the SDW. Leave the tarmac to follow the SDW left through the wooden fence and along the bridleway. **Keep straight ahead** at the wooden waymarker, staying on the SDW. Go through the gate and **take the left fork, staying on the SDW** to climb the steep little slope straight ahead. At the top of Amberley Mount, go through a gate. Pass the kissing gate to SSSI Springhead Estate and instead **walk straight ahead** on the SDW.

11 At the four-way wooden waymarker, **turn left** through the gate. Bear left to follow the bridleway along the ridge above the gully as you descend this steep slope. The path curves right. Go past (or through) the gate and continue straight ahead down the hill. Go through the gate to arrive at a busy road.

DIRECTIONS CONTINUE OVERLEAF ▶

AMBERLEY WILD BROOKS

12   Go **left** and then **very soon right** down Rackham Street. Pass Rackham Farmhouse on this lane. As you go through the houses, look out for the waymarker sign.

13   Walk **left** on the signed public footpath.

> ⟳ **SC**: or follow Rackham Street **straight ahead**, rejoining main route at point 15 or point 16.

Go **left again and right** following the path as it runs between fences and a wall. Cross the stile and **go straight ahead** across the open field. Cross the next stile and **walk left**, along the gently climbing lane.

14   Just before the house, **turn right** at the public footpath wooden waymarker. The track leads you diagonally across the field. You are doubling back on yourself but avoiding lane-walking. Cross a couple of footbridges, following the footpath to the stile ahead. **Turn left**, crossing the stile. **Walk straight ahead**, and follow the path over the next stile into the copse. Cross another stile and **go diagonally left** past Rackham Mill. Pass a wooden waymarker and cross another stile. Cross the footbridge and **follow the footpath left** along the edge of Rackham Plantation. The track curves to follow the boundary. Pass a couple of benches. At the wooden waymarker by the gate, **walk right** following the direction of the arrow on the waymarker post as the track curves through the wood. Go past the gate and arrive at the lane.

15   Walk **left** on this quiet lane. Pass Glebe Farm. **Reach the T-junction**, at the end of Greatham Road. (**Turn left** for Greatham Bridge, the car park at Waltham Brooks and Coldwaltham.) **Turn right** for Wiggonholt Common and main route through Pulborough Brooks. Walk up a slight hill. Pass two bridleways on your right and keep walking.

16   At the T-junction with the road to Rackham, **turn left** along the signed public footpath into the woods. This is Wiggonholt Heath, part of RSPB Pulborough Brooks Nature Reserve. Walk up the slight gradient on the sandy path amidst pine trees on one side and deciduous trees on the other. At the three-way wooden waymarker, take the **left fork**, which is the signed footpath. Climb the slope.

17 At the top, the RSPB Visitor Centre (cafe, shop, viewing point) and car park is to your left. **Walk straight ahead** on the footpath and then at the end of the fence, **double back and turn left**. Walk through the car park and across the driveway. Follow the footpath (which is beside the Visitor Centre) **straight ahead in the direction of the church. Keep straight ahead** following the waymarker sign. Cross the footbridge over the stream and the stile (boggy ground!). At the top of the hill, **turn right** at the wooden waymarker sign and cross the stile.

18 You are at Wiggonholt. **Turn left** to walk on the public footpath past the church. Cross the stile and **walk straight ahead** to the next stile. This stretch of path takes you across RSPB Pulborough Brooks land. There are hides off to right and left. Cross the stile and **walk straight ahead** across the field. **Head right** at the wooden waymarker sign and cross the stile. Walk **straight ahead**. Go through the gate and follow the signed footpath **straight ahead**. Go across another stile and follow the footpath **diagonally left**. Head for the raised bank and **turn right** at the wooden signpost. Walk along the banks of the River Arun. Cross the stile and **continue straight ahead** on the path. This is still the line of the old Roman causeway across the marsh. Walk straight ahead across the footbridge.

19 Leave the embankment to **follow the signed footpath straight across the field** to the red-roofed house. Go through the gate and follow the footpath **straight ahead**. At the end of Barn House Lane, **emerge in Pulborough**.

20 **Cross the road and walk diagonally right** to climb up Potts Lane opposite. At the top, **turn left** along the road. Where the road bends, **fork off left** to walk along Rectory Lane. This bridleway runs past various houses and offers a last view over the floodplain to the Downs. Pass the Chequers Hotel. **Cross the A29 and walk straight ahead** up Church Place, past St Mary's Church. **Turn left** along the signed footpath before the bridge over the railway line to retrace earlier footsteps.

CHALK ESCARPMENT, WOODLAND & CHANCTONBURY RING

DISTANCE: 12.4KM/7.7MILES » **TOTAL ASCENT:** 319M/1,046FT » **START GR:** TQ 122131 » **TIME:** ALLOW 4 HOURS
SATNAV: RH20 4AL » **MAP:** OS EXPLORER OL10, ARUNDEL & PULBOROUGH, 1:25,000 » **REFRESHMENTS:** FRANKLAND ARMS,
WASHINGTON, OR JUNGLE TEA ROOM, ASHINGTON » **NAVIGATION:** STRAIGHTFORWARD BUT CARE NEEDED IN POINT 8.

VIEW FROM CHANCTONBURY RING

11 Chalk Escarpment, Distinctive Woodland & Chanctonbury Ring

A steep climb to atmospheric Chanctonbury Ring followed by a leisurely woodland descent and easy meander back across grazing fields in full view of the Downs.

Washington » Chanctonbury Hill » Chanctonbury Ring » Court Plantation » Mouse Lane » Combe Holt » Washington

Start

Small car park at the entrance to Washington village, next to Washington Recreation Ground. GR: TQ 122131.

The Walk

Climb up to the Downs through the woodland. Fallen trees and gradients add an intensity and drama beyond prettiness. This woodland is unusual because it grows on a chalk escarpment. Chalk grassland, scrub and a dewpond add to the diversity of habitats and, consequently, Chanctonbury Hill is a Site of Special Scientific Interest. Breeding species include the protected great crested newt, downland birds (meadow pipit, corn bunting) and woodland birds (green woodpecker, nightingale).

The steep climb rewards you with the sensation of being up above the world. Join a fairly rough section of the South Downs Way and continue to climb steeply, passing tumuli. Once at the top, enjoy almost 360 degrees views over the intricate criss-crossings of fields, downland grazing and woodland. Look around you, knowing that almost everywhere is within your sights.

Chanctonbury Ring is a well-known landmark. The trees were planted in 1760 by Charles Goring, of Wiston House, and suffered terribly in the great storm of 1987. Chanctonbury Ring is named for the Iron Age fort beneath the trees. None would grow at its centre and, in 1908, the ruins of a small Roman temple were discovered there. This is without doubt an atmospheric location, steeped in history.

Descend through more atmospheric woodland, looking out for a ruined house. The final stretch of this walk contrasts nicely with the downland section but is best walked when the ground is dryer. A summer's day is the perfect time to enjoy these footpaths across peaceful fields beneath Chanctonbury Hill. Look out for the tramcar at Great Barn Farm!

Refreshment choices are limited. You may wish to drive to the Jungle Tea Room at Big Plant Nursery in nearby Ashington.

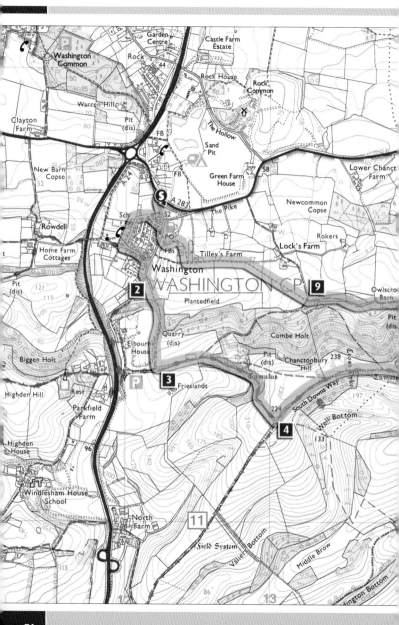

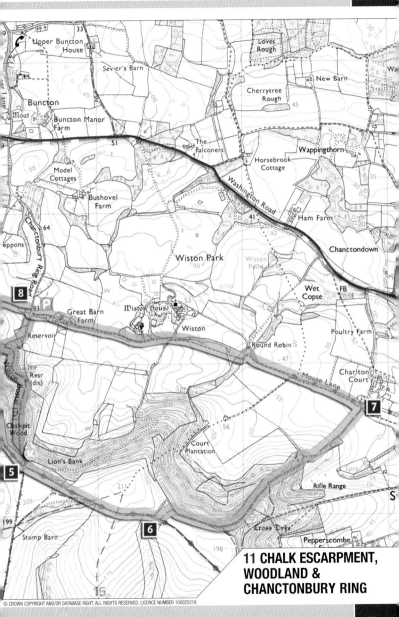

11 CHALK ESCARPMENT, WOODLAND & CHANCTONBURY RING

Directions – Chalk Escarpment, Distinctive Woodland & Chanctonbury Ring

❶ Walk along the road into Washington and **turn right** on to the signed tarmac footpath. Join the road and continue straight ahead, past the play area. Follow the lane round and up past the school. **Turn left** at the top of School Lane. At the end of The Street, **turn right** on to a busy road. Pass the bus stop.

2 Opposite Stocks Mead, **turn left**, taking the signed off-road shortcut to the South Downs Way (SDW). Go through gates and head diagonally across the field, following waymarks. Cross the stile and climb a few steep steps on to the woodland path ahead. Follow the track straight up past the field.

3 **Turn left, joining the SDW**. Keep left at a fork. Stay on the chalk and flint SDW, ignoring a couple of bridleway offshoots. It's a steep climb to the top.

4 **Turn left** at the wooden waymarker/three-way junction to stay on the SDW. Pass the noticeboard near the dewpond. Chanctonbury Ring is an open access area so walks around the ancient monument are allowed. **Stay on the signposted SDW** to follow our route, following the SDW through Findon Park Farm. Pass Chanctonbury Ring and hill fort. Continue on along the track, passing through the open gateway and downwards. Pass a bridleway.

5 At the corner junction of paths and signpost, **continue straight ahead** on the SDW.

> **SC**: By the signpost, it is possible to **go left** down Wiston Bostall through Chalkpit Wood. Follow the track past the reservoir to the car park on Chanctonbury Ring Road, rejoining the main route at point 8.

A bridleway joins the main route. Continue straight ahead.

6 **Turn left** at the wooden signpost to *Steyning*. By the trees, follow the bridleway marker **right** to go around the wood. **Stay left** where the bridleway forks, heading down into the trees. Follow the wide, chalk track down through the trees. At the junction, keep walking **straight ahead** on the same bridleway. Notice the hidden ruined house on the left near the gate with views to Steyning. Stay on this woodland bridleway, **keeping left** at the fork. At the next fork, **go right**, staying on the woodland bridleway.

The path soon comes to the edge of a field. Keep walking **straight ahead**. At the gap in the hedge, walk right slightly to where the path continues between two hedges.

7 At the waymarker, **go left**, climbing the small steps to walk along the footpath. You are now walking parallel with Mouse Lane with views to the Downs on your left. By the gate, **keep straight ahead** on the public footpath. At the end of the field, **head left and then almost immediately right** past a marker post and through the copse to keep following the footpath in the same direction. Cross the stile to continue **straight ahead**. Cross another stile and continue on the fenced path. The path joins the lane beside the private grounds of Wiston House. **Turn left** to keep walking west. Notice the small footbridge over the lane. Walk on past the sign for *Chanctonbury* as the track turns to mud and stone, climbing gently upwards. Follow the track through Great Barn Farm buildings. Notice the raised granary. Look out for the tramcar.

8 Reach the lane. This is Chanctonbury Ring Road, with the Wiston Bostal bridleway to your left, car park to your right. **Turn right** very briefly and then left in order to **continue straight ahead on the bridleway**. Follow the track into the wood. Go through a gate and continue, climbing slightly as you skirt around the base of Chanctonbury. Stay on this path as it becomes wooded.

9 Emerge from the wood. Notice the marker post and go right through the gate and follow the footpath **diagonally** across the field. Go through a gate into the next field. Continue past a signpost and walk on through a gateway and along beside a fence. Pass metal gates and a **few metres further on, turn right** over the stile and follow the footpath straight ahead past the house. Go over another stile and walk **diagonally left**. Cross another stile and path to follow the narrow footpath opposite, concealed behind a hedge. Cross a footbridge and head **diagonally right** to clamber over one last stile. Emerge on the road in Washington. **Turn right** to go past the pub and return to the car park.

BRAMBER & BEEDING HILL

DISTANCE: 12.6KM/7.8MILES » **TOTAL ASCENT:** 329M/1,079FT » **START GR:** BRAMBER TQ 188107; BEEDING HILL TQ 207096 » **TIME:** ALLOW 4 HOURS » **SATNAV:** BRAMBER BN44 3WU; BEEDING HILL BN43 5FH » **MAP:** OS EXPLORER OL11, BRIGHTON & HOVE, 1:25,000 » **REFRESHMENTS:** THE CASTLE INN HOTEL OR THE OLD TOLLGATE, BRAMBER; THE KING'S HEAD OR THE RISING SUN, UPPER BEEDING » **NAVIGATION:** STRAIGHTFORWARD.

ST MARY'S HOUSE, BRAMBER

12 Bramber & Beeding Hill: Town & Downland Loop

12.6km/7.8miles

A figure-of-eight circuit looping through Bramber and Upper Beeding to climb Beeding Hill and reach a small but satisfying downland loop, before descending to follow the Downs Link back.

Bramber » St Mary's House » Castle Town » Beeding Hill » Room Bottom » Tottington Barn » Bushy Bottom » Beeding Hill » Downs Link » Bramber

Start

The Street car park (no charge) opposite the Castle Inn Hotel in Bramber. GR: TQ 188107.

Alternative Start

Beeding Hill Car Park. GR: TQ 207096.

The Walk

Walk along the historic high street. St Mary's House, built circa 1470, is open on selected afternoons. Take a scenic detour through meadowland and along the river. Look out for distant Beeding Hill beckoning before returning to the High Street. This is the only walk included in this guide with a 'road' section but it is recommended by a woman walker I know who regularly uses it as a circuit when training for the South Downs Trek.

Walk up the peaceful bridleway to Beeding Hill. It's quite a climb, but it's easy to appreciate the peace and quiet once on this beautiful, semi-shaded track. At the top, absorb interesting views towards the cement works chimneys, Lancing College and the sea. Continue on the downland loop or choose to descend.

The small downland loop is mainly off the South Downs Way (SDW) and incorporates a variety of tracks. The first bridleway is narrow with a 'cutting' feel, birds darting out of the undergrowth. Emerge from the tunnel of trees to enjoy far-reaching views over Steyning and farmland. Walk through the wildlife site in summer and downland butterflies flicker fast and bright.

Touch base with the SDW, ramble down an easy, well-surfaced bridleway and turn on to a chalk stretch of Monarch's Way. The path is narrow, yet spectacular in its own small way, dipping and climbing between grazing fields, then back up Beeding Hill. Descend on the SDW, following it to Botolphs, the point where it crosses the Downs Link. The easy Downs Link leads you back to Bramber. Options for refreshments vary: The Old Tollgate Hotel has a carvery restaurant and may serve cream teas in the garden during summer. The Castle Inn Hotel is a free house with a restaurant, bar menu and a large terrace at the rear.

12 BRAMBER & BEEDING HILL

Directions – Bramber & Beeding Hill

⊙→ **Turn left** out of the car park along The Street. Pass St Mary's House entrance and **turn right** along the signed footpath. Continue straight ahead past a signpost and through the metal gate by the entrance to the caravan park. Soon, the footpath **turn right** towards the road. Follow the path all the way to the gate. Go through it and walk straight ahead. Head towards the chimney and then veer left and, before you reach a stony bridleway, turn and, keeping left of the tree, walk towards the houses. Emerge on the banks of the River Adur. **Turn left** to return to reach the High Street walking along the river bank.

2 **Turn right** when you reach the High Street, walking over the footbridge and into Upper Beeding. Pass the King's Head. Walk along this road, passing flint houses and walls and the village hall. At the mini-roundabout, go straight on past the garage. At the busy roundabout where the Rising Sun pub is **take the Henfield Road left**. Continue past Towers School and Manor Road.

3 **Turn right** along the public bridleway/private road *The Bostal*.

4 Continue up the hill past a bridleway and keep a steady pace up this steep slope.

5 Beside Beeding Hill Car Park, you have a choice:

　　⊙→ **SC: Turn right** to return to Bramber via The Downs Link.

Or **turn left** to follow the downland loop, taking the narrow bridleway to the left of the National Trust sign. Follow the narrow bridleway past a signpost, ignoring the steps.

6 At the marker post **go right**, towards a signpost. Go through a gate, entering the Site of Special Scientific Interest protected wildlife site. Follow the track up straight ahead, keeping roughly parallel with the fence. At the top, **turn left at the signpost** and walk along the footpath. Follow the track **straight ahead**. See (and hear) the scrambling centre below. Go through the gate and pass a marker post. Walk along parallel with the fence. **Turn right** at the marker post and go through two gates. Pass a marker post and go through a gate.

7   **Turn left** along the South Downs Way (SDW) for a short distance. Pass the youth hostel and Truleigh House. At the path crossroads and signpost, **turn right** along the easy walking bridleway.

8   At the gate and marker post, **turn right** along Monarch's Way, following an undulating gravel bridleway. Go through several gates and continue straight ahead. Before long you will be back at Beeding Hill.

9   At the four-way marker post by the car park, go through the gate to follow the SDW **diagonally left** down the field. See the chimney from the old cement works, Lancing College and the sea to your left. Go through the gate and down a narrow track.

10   At the road, **go left** for a very short distance. Pass the bus stops. Cross the road with care and **turn right** into a lay-by to folllow the SDW sign. Pass a tap and stone trough. This is Botolphs where the SDW and the Downs Link cross. Cross the bridge over the River Adur.

11   **Follow the Downs Link right**. See Bramber Castle ahead. Follow the Downs Link away from the river. At the signpost, **turn right** towards towards Henfield, staying on the Downs Link to the busy A283. Keep going, all the way back to Bramber. Emerge at the roundabout. **Turn right** to return to your car.

DEVIL'S DYKE VERSUS SECRETS OF LOW-LYING FOOTPATHS

DISTANCE: 10.4KM/6.5MILES » **TOTAL ASCENT:** 306M/1,005FT » **START GR:** TQ 247114 » **TIME:** ALLOW 5 HOURS
SATNAV: BN5 9LU » **MAP:** OS EXPLORER OL11, BRIGHTON & HOVE, 1:25,000 » **REFRESHMENTS:** THE SHEPHERD AND
DOG, FULKING; DEVIL'S DYKE INN, DEVIL'S DYKE; THE ROYAL OAK, POYNINGS » **NAVIGATION:** CARE NEEDED IN PARTS OF
LOW SECTION.

A DOWNLAND TRACK NEAR FULKING HILL

13 Spectacular Devil's Dyke Versus Secrets of Low-Lying Footpaths

(Can be split into two shorter 3½ mile walks)

A balance between exploring the popular downland area around Devil's Dyke and the lesser-known nearby footpaths beyond Poynings, Fulking and Edburton with a choice of pubs en route.

Fulking » Edburton » Edburton Hill » Fulking Hill » Devil's Dyke » Poynings » Fulking

Start

By the village tap and memorial in honour of John Ruskin. Roadside parking in Fulking just beyond The Shepherd and Dog, heading out of the village towards Edburton. Walk back into Fulking, up Stammers Hill. GR: TQ 247114.

The Walk

Footpaths on the low section of this walk appear less used and may be poorly maintained, or run through crop fields. Your pay-off is the chance to discover some well-kept secrets. Imagine no noise but the swash of crops around your ankles, unobtrusive birdsong and the echo of bees. As you wander through vibrant meadows of wild flowers and waving grass, crickets hop with your every footstep. A twig snaps and you turn to discover that you're being watched by a deer. All this with the added bonus of the Downs as a backdrop!

The sight of Edburton Hill may be daunting but don't worry, there are steps, albeit steep and uneven. They lead on to the National Trust Fulking Escarpment where a gradient gives the land a wildness and character that more gentle slopes may lack.

From the top, trace your steps back past the garage, the line of the hedge and the copse to give some scale to the extensive views before you. Join a busy stretch of chalk and flint South Downs Way where cattle often graze. Detour to the picturesque Shepherd and Dog to enjoy lunch in a ringside location or wait and visit the welcoming Royal Oak at Poynings.

Was Devil's Dyke made by he himself in an attempt to dig a ditch through the Downs and flood the churches? The place is awash with legends and history, as popular today as it ever was. Hang gliders up in the air, kite flyers down on the ground. Mountain bikers and walkers, families and tourists. This is a place where people gather. There's an Iron Age fort, busy pub, bus stop, orbing, zorbing, sphering. In the past there's been a steep-grade railway, a cable car, an amusement park and plans for the seventh wonder of the world, but forget all that and look at the landscape. It is, as it ever was, simply stunning and that's what draws people here.

13 DEVIL'S DYKE VERSUS SECRETS OF LOW-LYING FOOTPATHS

Directions – Devil's Dyke Versus Secrets of Low-Lying Footpaths

❺ By the village tap and roadside memorial, **walk left** on the footpath. Ignore the park and head to signpost and kissing gate in the right corner. Go **straight ahead** across the field. Cross two stiles to traverse the small field. **Walk left and then diagonally right** through the field. Cross the concrete track and continue straight ahead through the gate on the signed footpath. Go through a gate, cross a bridge over a stream and **walk left**, as signed through grazing field.

2 Cross the footbridge and go through a kissing gate to **continue straight ahead**. At the next kissing gate and bridge, **continue straight ahead**, ignoring the bridleway leading off right.

3 At the next wooden waymarker, observe the footpath sign going **diagonally left** and follow it across the field with a hedge on the left. In the corner, walk past an overgrown waymarker and **left** across the bridge. Walk straight ahead along the footpath past a sign and houses. Go **left** at the bridge and pass a signpost to walk on towards the Downs. At the marker post, **turn briefly left and then right** along a driveway/footpath to reach the road.

4 At the road, **go left** briefly (see Springs' Smokery) and **then right** up the public footpath. Head through the car park and **walk right** up the flight of wooden steps (!). The steps lead on to a narrow path and stile which in turn leads you to Fulking Escarpment. **Walk left** and enjoy the sweeping views. **Take care** on the rough, narrow path as there's a steep drop to the left. Cross the stile and continue climbing to the top. At the bridleway, **walk right**.

5 Go through the gate and follow the **South Downs Way left**.

6 Where you see Fulking village to the left, look out for the marker post. **Take the narrow chalk footpath leading diagonally left**. This narrow, stony path runs between two banks.

7 At the marker post, you have a choice. To continue on our **main route to Poynings: Follow the chalk bridleway right**. Or take a shortcut:

  ☺ SC: To return directly to Fulking, **walk left** at the marker post.

Back on the main route. The chalk bridleway becomes grassy and runs beside a steep drop. At the top, leave the Fulking Escarpment, to **go left** through the gate. Join the path heading left towards the Devil's Dyke Inn.

8 At the pub, walk in front of the car park and pick up the **footpath signed straight ahead** at the far end. **Go straight ahead** at the marker post. Follow the ridge round to the right. **Turn left** to go across the stile and **head diagonally right** down the hill. The path becomes chalky and heads left into the trees. Go through the gate into the woods and keep following the path. **Turn right** along the fence as you leave Devil's Dyke. Emerge on a path between houses. At the end of the bridleway (Dykes Lane), **go right** towards the pub.

9 **Turn left** into the pub car park and and find the path which leaves the driveway between buildings and the car park. Walk down a concrete track. Go through a kissing gate and go straight ahead past the signpost. Go through a gate and across a stream. At the marker post, in sight of the lane, **turn left** along the footpath. Walk along beside the fence.

10 At the end of the path, **walk left** along Mill Lane. This track wends between gardens and houses. After passing the water treatment tank, cross the stile and **continue straight ahead**. Pass the pond on your left. Keep walking across the field. Go over the stile and **straight ahead** across the field. There's no obvious path but you're heading for the stile on the opposite fence. **Bear right slightly** and head for the gate, which is halfway along the opposite boundary. Cross the stile.

11 **Walk right** along the lane for a short way. After the bridge, **go left** over the stile and along the footpath through a clearing. **Cross the bridge** over the stream and follow the narrow path ahead.

12 At the marker post, **walk left** across the bridge. Cross the stile, **bear left** and **follow the fence straight ahead** to the corner. Cross two stiles and **walk straight ahead** towards the Downs. Cross the stile in the corner of the field and a second stile straight ahead. Cross the 'lane' and over a third stile. **Walk straight ahead** across the field. Cross the stile in the corner. You are coming into Fulking. **Head right** along the footpath through the gate. Follow the footpath across the field back to our start point (path may not be obvious due to crops). Cross the stile. Pass the children's play area. Go straight ahead to the gate and **turn right** at the road to return to the pub.

THE HEART OF THE HISTORIC DOWNLANDS

DISTANCE: 14KM/8.7MILES » **TOTAL ASCENT:** 506M/1,660FT » **START GR:** TQ 300140 » **TIME:** ALLOW 5.5 HOURS
SATNAV: BN6 9PJ » **MAP:** OS EXPLORER OL11, BRIGHTON & HOVE, 1:25,000 » **REFRESHMENTS:** JACK & JILL, CLAYTON; THE
PLOUGH OR WAYFIELD PARK FARM SHOP, PYECOMBE; WILDFLOUR CAFE, SADDLESCOMBE FARM (CLOSED ON MONDAYS);
DEVIL'S DYKE INN, DEVIL'S DYKE; THE ROYAL OAK, POYNINGS » **NAVIGATION:** STRAIGHTFORWARD, BUT THERE ARE NO
WAYMARKERS OR SIGNS BETWEEN PYECOMBE AND SADDLESCOMBE.

NEWTIMBER CHURCH

14 The Heart of the Historic Downlands

14km/8.7miles

A hike around the beautiful areas of Newtimber and Saddlescombe with the chance to explore Bronze Age Wolstonbury Hill and legendary Devil's Dyke.

Clayton » Wellcombe Bottom » Pyecombe » Newtimber Hill » Saddlescombe » Devil's Dyke » Pyecombe » Round Hill » Wolstonbury » Ashen Plantation » Clayton

Start

Clayton Recreation Ground car park (no charge), Underhill Lane, opposite the church. Can be busy at weekends. Or park in Hassocks (or come by train!) and use the footpath running between Butcher's Wood and the railway line: see route 15 (page 99) for details. GR: TQ 300140.

The Walk

A friend told me about Saddlescombe as her favourite dog walking haunt, and I expanded our route to explore this central, historic area of the Downs. A bit of climbing enables you to enjoy this undulating terrain. Despite being easily accessible, the walk has a real 'National Park' feel to it.

From Pyecombe, climb to the edge of ancient woodland, Newtimber Holt, cared for by the National Trust. Newtimber Hill is known for its chalk grassland providing a rich habitat for downland flowers and insects, including rarities like the silver spotted skipper, burnt orchid, red star thistle and juniper tree. From the brow of Newtimber Hill, pause to admire the views over Saddlescombe towards Devil's Dyke.

Saddlescombe Farm was at one time owned by the Knights Templar. *A South Downs Farm in the 1860s*, by Maude Robinson, evokes more recent history. You can still see the famous donkey wheel but, luckily, the poor donkey no longer has to tread the boards to draw well water for the thirsty farm labourer. Nowadays, there's a drinking tap beside the South Downs Way, but we recommend that you stop at the Wildflour Cafe in the converted barn at Saddlescombe Farm.

Climb the legendary Devil's Dyke (see route 13) and descend past the concrete remains of the cable car. Down through the copse to Poynings, past the well-loved Royal Oak pub. Return across fields, passing the often forgotten historic Newtimber Church. Scramble beyond the chalk pits up towards spectacular Wolstonbury Hill, diverting to explore the 'fort'. It's unusual in that the ditch is inside the ramparts, leading some to speculate that the Bronze Age enclosure had a peaceful purpose.

14 THE HEART OF THE HISTORIC DOWNLANDS

Directions – The Heart of the Historic Downlands

❻ From the car park, **head diagonally left** across the field to the **kissing gate**. Cross New Road and the A273. **Turn left** down New Way Lane by the Jack & Jill Inn.

2 **Turn left** up the waymarked public bridleway. You are walking to the side of National Trust Wolstonbury Hill. Climb this steep stretch of wooded path. **Ignore** a stile leading right. Pass a gate. At the top of the hill, pass another gate and **continue straight ahead past the signed crossroads** along the bridleway. After a short distance, reach another signpost and **turn right and climb over a stile**. **Head diagonally left** along the footpath, which may not be immediately obvious, enjoying hilltop vistas. Cross the stile and **continue in the same direction, diagonally right**. The last section descends steeply through scrub. Climb over a stile and **continue in a similar direction** across the next field. Look for a signpost a short distance from the corner. Go through the kissing gate and **turn right** passing the barn. Walk to the end of the drive and past Manor Barn. **Turn left**.

3 You are at one end of Pyecombe village.

▶**OR** Walk left to the end of the road for the Plough at Pyecombe.

Back on the main route: **turn right briefly to walk across the bridge** over the A23 and **walk straight ahead and pass Wayfield Park Farm Shop. Climb up** the narrow track running alongside the fence. The path continues upwards through a grazing field. At the signpost, follow the hedge-lined bridleway **straight ahead**. Go through the gate. You are now on Newtimber Hill (National Trust). **Keep straight ahead** on the track between grazing fields and trees which mark the edge of Newtimber Holt.

4 **Turn sharp right** at the marker post to follow the bridleway. At the fence, **turn left** (without crossing the stile). Climb the slope, **turn right** through the gate and immediately **go left to continue walking in the same direction. Go straight ahead** over the brow of the hill, ignoring the gate and following the natural path downwards. Saddlescombe is straight ahead. Walk on, past a marker post, along the line of the fence. Follow the path through a gate and continue down to the bottom. At the signpost, **turn right** through a gate joining the South Downs Way (SDW). **Walk along a stony track** through farm buildings.

5 You are in Saddlescombe. **Walk left** through the farm, nipping into the Information Barn and Wildflour Cafe. **Take the left fork** to continue on our main route to Devil's Dyke.

> **SC**: Direct to Poynings. Take the **right fork**, cross the road and go through the gate opposite to follow the tarmac bridleway. After the curve, **follow the footpath diagonally left** leaving the tarmac behind. Follow the track **right and then on through the trees** and cross the stile to continue on in the same direction. **Turn right** at the bridleway. Pass a marker post. At the waymarker, **go left** to follow the footpath. Pass a pond and, by the stile, head right across the open (bonfire) field to a stile and gate. Walk on through the garage and **at the lane, turn left**. At the wooden waymarker before the pub, **go right**. Go to the signpost at the start of point 7.

Cross the road, **head left** and follow the wooden waymarker signs for the SDW bridleway. Go through the gate and on to National Trust Summer Down, part of Devil's Dyke Estate. Follow the path right and see Poynings down below. Towards the top of this slope there's a broken marker post and the track forks. They do merge later but I suggest **taking the left fork**. Soon, pass beside a small car park. Continue on the path, up and through the scrubland. Ignore the gate to the road and continue on this track. Go through the gate and follow the bridleway straight ahead, as signed on the marker post. The deep, narrow valley to your right is Devil's Dyke. Continue in this direction alongside the deep narrow valley for some time. Pass a marker post with a small SDW sign and **continue straight ahead**. Cross the stile or go through the gate to reach the road.

6 **Turn right** along the road briefly towards Poynings and the Devil's Dyke pub. **Turn right** at the gate, following the bridleway along the 'other' edge of the valley. Pass the concrete remains of the cable car and see a matching one on the opposite side. Reach the gate. Spot distant Saddlescombe Farm on your right. The track curves round left through a gate and into the woods. Stay on this track, ignoring offshoot on left. At the small NT *Devil's Dyke* sign by the fence, **turn right**. Emerge on a path between houses. At the end of the bridleway (Dykes lane), **go right** to reach the pub.

DIRECTIONS CONTINUE OVERLEAF

7 Find the footpath which leaves the pub driveway by a marker post. Walk down a concrete track. Go through a kissing gate and continue straight ahead to the signpost (where OR joins). Go through a gate and across a stream. At the waymarker post continue straight on. At the lane **turn left and cross the road to immediately turn right** following the signed footpath opposite, passing the old school which is now a nursery. Cross the stile and **walk straight ahead**, although there's no obvious path. Newtimber Hill is on your right. Cross the stile in the corner of the field. After the timber footbridge, **head diagonally right** to the far gate. Cross the stile and **go left**. The footpath leads straight across the field. Cross the stile to join the road.

8 Negotiate the roundabout to follow the footpath signed **diagonally opposite**. Cross the stile and **walk diagonally right** to another stile. Walk along the fenced path **diagonally left**. At the end of the fence, continue across the stony driveway and through two gates. Walk straight on, **following the track left** at the end of the hedge. **Go right** at the stile.

9 **Turn left** along the lane. Pass the Old School House on your right. **Walk right** towards Newtimber Church along the public footpath. Head diagonally past the church to the gate. After the gate, **walk left**. Walk straight ahead at the gap/stile, heading right along the hedge to the noisy A23. Cross the stile and follow the track. At the slip road, **go right and then left through the underpass**. Follow the old road upwards. **Turn right** at the footpath sign. Soon, **turn left**, crossing the stile. Follow the track up past the fenced-off, working chalk pits. The slope is grassy and a steep climb in places with mud footholds. Go through a kissing gate.

10 Go **left** at the bridleway **then immediately right** to follow the footpath through the gate. You are back on National Trust Wolstonbury Hill. Digress to explore if you wish. Otherwise, **head diagonally left** towards the distant marker post. There are great views over the Weald to distant downland and, nearer at hand, to Danny House. At the copse, **keep straight ahead**, walking across the slope to follow the footpath before you. Follow the track down through the woods. Cross a couple of stiles and **turn right** on to the mud bridleway. Almost immediately, join another bridleway where you **turn right** at the marker post. Follow the path as it curves left. Take it steady up the hill and through the gate. Emerging into the light, see Jack and Jill windmills straight ahead. Go through the gate and **turn left**.

▷OR◁ Ignore the stile and stay on the mud and stone track doubling back slightly. Walk on, passing through the gate and on to a driveway. **Turn right** along New Way Lane (occasional fast traffic!).

To walk a shorter distance along New Way Lane, **turn right** at the stile. Follow the public footpath across the field to the stile, passing a signpost in the middle. Cross the stile across the fence, **turn left** and walk along the rough path to the gate. **Turn left** on to the bridleway from the start of your walk and descend. **Turn right** along New Way Lane. **Turn right** at the A273 and cross both roads carefully to walk through the gate/stile and back across the park to your car.

GATEWAY TO THE DOWNS
DISTANCE: 14.3KM/8.9MILES » **TOTAL ASCENT:** 290M/951FT » **START GR:** TQ 304155 » **TIME:** ALLOW 5 HOURS
SATNAV: BN6 8JD » **MAP:** OS EXPLORER OL11, BRIGHTON & HOVE, 1:25,000 » **REFRESHMENTS:** THE PURPLE CARROT AT
NO6, PROPER CYCLING AND COFFEE OR BELLA & MEG'S CAFE, HASSOCKS; THE BULL, THE WHITE HORSE INN, THE NUTMEG TREE
OR THE GREEN WELLY, DITCHLING » **NAVIGATION:** PATHS UNSIGNED IN WELLCROFT SHAW WOOD.

WESTMESTON BOSTALL

15 Gateway to the Downs: Windmills, Ditchling Beacon & Downland Villages

14.3km/8.9miles

Rural paths across fields, through woodland and the historic village of Ditchling are joined by an exhilarating stretch of the South Downs Way along the ridge between Jack and Jill windmills and Ditchling Beacon.

Hassocks » Jack & Jill windmills » Ditchling Beacon » Westmeston » Ditchling » Oldlands Mill » Hassocks

Start

Brick pillars to footpath signed to South Downs National Park, near railway bridge crossing B2116/Keymer Road through Hassocks. GR: TQ 304155.

Park at Dale Avenue car park in Hassocks (SATNAV: BN6 8LN). Or from Hassocks Station leave via ticket office side and descend via stone steps to B2116, walk under the brick bridge and cross the road.

The Walk

Hassocks, with its railway station, is ideally situated as a gateway to the Downs. Walk past Woodland Trust's Butcher's Wood and across grazing fields to the waiting Downs. Climb through Clayton and up a steep footpath, to the windmills. Jill, a nineteenth century corn windmill, has been successfully restored, while Jack is a private residence. The sight of the windmills' sails silhouetted on the horizon signifies that you have almost reached the crest of the hill.

This dramatic chalk and flint stretch of the South Downs Way runs along a ridge offering downland vistas right towards Brighton and the sea and, left, over classic hedged fields, Wealden villages and woodland. See Burnt House dewpond and,

by Ditchling Beacon, Sussex Wildlife Trust's Nature Reserve can be accessed left from the South Downs Way.

Rest a while as you begin your steep descent. This butterfly-magnet slope is more peaceful than Beacon viewpoints. The ground at Westmeston Bostall may be rough, uneven and steep (!) but the chalk paths give the downland gradients a real beauty. There's a bench near the bottom too. From Westmeston, take lesser-used paths across meadows strewn with wild flowers, fields where elegant horses graze, and on through farms and woods.

Meander through the Arts and Crafts village of Ditchling. Walk past 'Sopers', home of letter-cutter, wood-engraver, sculptor and type designer Eric Gill. The house became a centre for the local artistic community: find out more when you pass Ditchling Museum. There's a good choice of teashops and pubs. To return to Hassocks, choose between the friendly Greyhound pub and grassy footpaths, or mainly hard-surfaced tracks past Oldland Mill. Whichever way you go, the Downs form the perfect backdrop to your journey.

JILL WINDMILL

**15 GATEWAY
TO THE DOWNS**

Directions – Gateway to the Downs

⑤→ From the entrance to the footpath signed to the South Downs National Park, walk up some steps to the 'Cinder Path', which runs alongside the railway line. Ignore offshoot paths. Pass Butcher's Wood entrance.

> **OR** If you wish, divert through entrance to the Woodland Trust site Butcher's Wood, which is well worth a wander, especially in bluebell season. A network of unmarked paths should either bring you back out further up the Cinder Path or on the field just beyond point 2.

2 **Turn left** over a stile at the end of Butcher's Wood. Follow the path **diagonally right** across a field. Continue on past a signpost between undergrowth and woods. Cross a stile and **turn right**. Continue **straight ahead** on this track towards the Downs.

3 Cross a stile and the B2112 and continue **straight ahead** through the gate along the bridleway. Walk past a pond and on to a brick driveway. Follow the gravel path **straight ahead**. It joins with Spring Lane, passing several houses. Hit Underhill Lane where you walk **left** up the hill for a very short distance.

4 Look for a wooden-waymarked footpath heading **right** into a wood just before the South East Water property. It's steep! Start climbing. Cross the stile and follow the chalky footpath straight ahead. Emerge into an open field with no obvious path. Go **straight ahead** and then **left** to climb up the field on the footpath which runs beside the fence. Soon you will see the Jack and Jill windmills.

5 Pass the Jack and Jill car park on your right. Go through a wooden gate in front of you to follow public bridleway around the windmills. Emerge on to a stony, well-used path. Follow it **left** up the slope.

6 Towards the top of the hill, note the wooden waymarker at the junction of paths. Join the South Downs Way (SDW), following it **straight ahead** all the way to Ditchling Beacon. You will pass Burnt House dewpond, Keymer Post, and go through several gates before you reach the car park at Ditchling Beacon. **Cross the road** and continue **straight ahead** through the gate on the SDW.

7 Almost immediately, **go left** over the wooden stile. Follow the steep footpath which descends right. There are few level footholds and a very steep drop at the side of the path. Pass a wooden marker and then hit another chalk path. **Turn left** along this narrow and uneven path to the gate. Follow the path through the copse to another gate. Pass the entrance to Westmeston Farm, continuing **straight ahead** along the lane.

8 Reach the site of old Westmeston Village Well. Walk towards Ditchling but after the bus stop **bear left**, following the public footpath to Ditchling, which runs above the road for a while. Go down and up some steps. Cross a stile and follow a waymarked footpath. Walk through a meadow with views of the Downs to your left. Cross stile into next field, following direction of arrow and line of fence to your right. This is Westmeston Place: the path does not approach the pond and stables.

Cross a stile in the corner. Head **diagonally left** towards the stile and footbridge. Go through a tall kissing gate and walk along beside the fence. Go through another kissing gate and into some woods. Head **right** on the mud path. Easy to miss: at the marker post **bear right** past a fallen tree, along an unsigned path between trees and scrub. Continue **straight ahead** past a couple of marker posts. Cross a signed stile and footbridge to follow a narrow public footpath along the backs of gardens. Arrive in 'Shirley's' residential road. **Head diagonally right** to a wooden waymarker and walk along the narrow fenced footpath beside Odd Acre's driveway.

9 Cross the road and enter Ditchling Recreation Ground. Walk **diagonally left** and head to the left of Ditchling Pavilion. Continue **straight ahead** alongside the hedge. Walk around the tennis courts and **turn left** through a gate. Path becomes Farm Lane. At road, **turn right** along East End Lane. **Turn left** along Ditchling High Street. Cross the road and **turn right** up Church Lane, following brown *museum* sign. **Turn left** to go through graveyard then **right** down steps to village green and walk past Ditchling Museum of Art & Craft.

DIRECTIONS CONTINUE OVERLEAF

Directions – Gateway to the Downs
continued...

10 At duck pond, follow lane **right**. It curves left past Lodge Hill. Options:

Main Route via Greyhound pub (note: fields can be boggy when wet): Afte the fence, where the lane curves right, go **left** over the stile and follow the footpat **straight ahead**. Cross the stile and footbridge. Walk **straight ahead** and then lef at the signpost towards the kissing gate. Go through and walk **straight ahead** alon the track. Emerge on Silverdale. **Turn right** along Keymer Road, passing the churc and the Greyhound pub. **Turn left** along Lodge Lane. Pass the private road. Cross Dal Avenue and almost immediately **turn right** along the wooden waymarked footpath.

Follow the footpath as it **turns left and then right**. At the marker post, **wal diagonally** across the school playing field staying left of the hedge. Head into th copse and cross the footbridge. Follow the footpath **diagonally** across the field through the gap and keep going in the same direction across the next field. Cross th planked stile and walk **right** along the hedge, parallel with the Downs. At the secon gate, recognise the shingle track and path from earlier in your walk (point 2) and **tur right** along the grassy footpath. **Go left** over the stile by the driveway. Follow th track across the field towards the railway line. Cross the stile and **turn right** on t the Cinder Path. Walk past Butcher's Wood to emerge on Keymer Road in Hassocks.

▶OR via Oldland Mill (more hard-surfaced tracks): Follow lane **right** as it curve and climbs past Lodge Hill, ignoring several stiles/steps. At the top of the hil **go left** across the stile. Take path **right** across top of sloping field. Cross stil and follow path. Go through gap and turn **left** towards Oldlands Mill. Follov tarmac path downhill to the road. Cross and walk **right**, heading out o Hassocks. At wooden waymarker, turn **left** on to footpath. Go through gate and follow track **straight ahead** and past another gate. Follow the path roun to the left where it comes into a new housing estate. Follow it down and **right** t the bridge which leads into Woodlands Road. Reach the mini roundabou where you turn **left** for Hassocks Village and right for the station.

CLOUDY VIEW BEYOND DITCHLING BEACON

SECTION 3

East Sussex

Walk by the sea on blustery cliffs past fragile lighthouses and grazing sheep. Absorb wide-open vistas and shady forest paths. Climb through heathland and up beyond agricultural fields to downland ridges and beacons where the world opens up before you. Enjoy the space.

VIEW TOWARDS SEVEN SISTERS, FROM NEAR BEACHY HEAD

AGRICULTURAL WEALD, PUBS & DOWNLAND TO DITCHLING BEACON

DISTANCE: 19.5KM/12.1MILES » **TOTAL ASCENT:** 488M/1,601FT » **START GR:** TQ 364161 » **TIME:** ALLOW 7-8 HOURS
SATNAV: BN7 3BW » **MAP:** OS EXPLORER OL11, BRIGHTON & HOVE, 1:25,000 » **REFRESHMENTS:** HALF MOON, PLUMPTON;
SEASONAL ICE CREAM VAN AT DITCHLING BEACON; THE JOLLY SPORTSMAN, EAST CHILTINGTON » **NAVIGATION:**
STRAIGHTFORWARD.

FOOTPATH ACROSS AGRICULTURAL FIELDS

16 Agricultural Weald, Pubs & Downland to Ditchling Beacon

This figure-of-eight walk runs through the agricultural weald, past a pleasant country pub to climb to more remote downland, before taking in high point, honeypot and nature reserve Ditchling Beacon, and a return back past the pub along more quiet agricultural tracks and a 'foodie' pub.

Plumpton Station at Plumpton Green » Plumpton Racecourse » Plumpton Agricultural College » Half Moon at Plumpton » Streat Hill » Bow Hill » Highpark Wood » Ditchling Beacon » Western Brow » Streat Hill » Plumpton » East Chiltington » Plumpton Green

Start

Plumpton Station.
Roadside parking. GR: TQ 364161.

The Walk

This walk is an interesting mixture of agricultural thoroughfares and downland exploration. It can be done in its entirety, split into two shorter walks or linked with the Hassocks walk (p99) to provide a linear station-to-station walk. Start from Plumpton Station and meander alongside the racecourse. During the first part of this walk, the Downs constantly draw the eye to the horizon: they are no less impressive because they're at a distance.

Plumpton is at the heart of agricultural Sussex and this route leads you through the grounds of the Agricultural College. During WWII, over 2,000 Land Army Girls trained here. A footpath obligingly leads you to the Half Moon pub at Plumpton. What better way to come upon a country pub with downland views than through a rough meadow of wild flowers?

Enjoy the steep climb as the mainly hard-surfaced Plumpton Bostall leads you up on to the Downs. The track transports you into another world where downland peace and tranquility is only interrupted by swooping birds, grazing cows and buzzing flies. Bountiful views too.

The beginning of this downland loop is on lesser-used, surprisingly remote paths. There's one stunning spot in particular where trees cluster on the slopes and the ground sweeps away towards the sky. Leave it to climb through crackling woodland. The paths become busier as you head for Ditchling Beacon. At 248 metres, this is the third highest point in the South Downs National Park, offering extensive views over the Weald. Ditchling Beacon is also the site of an Iron Age fort and, from the top plateau, there's access to the Sussex Wildlife Trust chalk grassland and scrub nature reserve on the steep northern slope. Return along the stunning ridge-top South Downs Way, and via peaceful East Chiltington where you may choose to drop in at the 'foodie' pub.

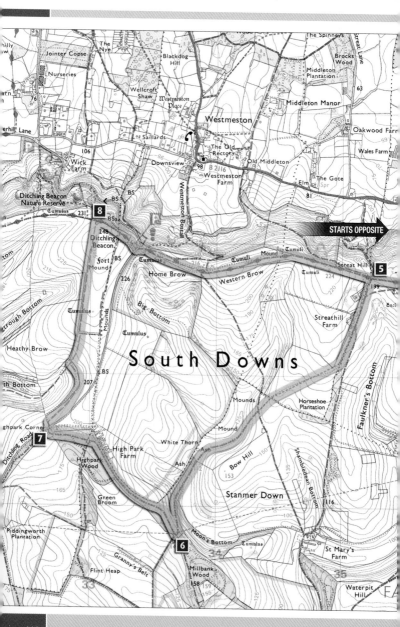

STARTS OPPOSITE

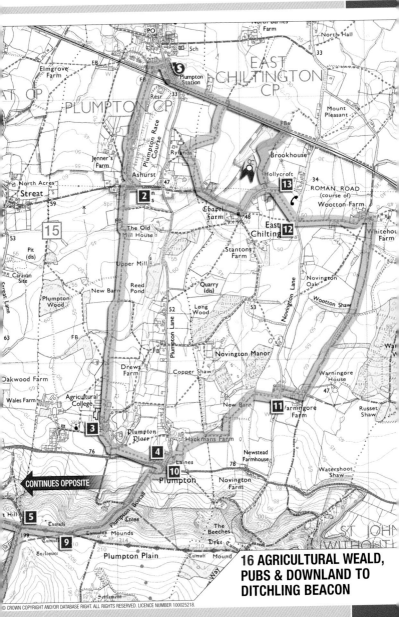

CONTINUES OPPOSITE

16 AGRICULTURAL WEALD, PUBS & DOWNLAND TO DITCHLING BEACON

Directions – Agricultural Weald, Pubs & Downland to Ditchling Beacon

❺ Emerge from Plumpton Station and **turn left** on to Station Road. Next, **turn left** int East View Fields. **Easy to miss: turn left** on to a footpath between numbers 14 an 16. **Cross the footbridge** over the railway line and walk straight ahead on the fence footpath between the racecourse and car park. The footpath becomes a tarmac driv beside the racecourse (so will be busy on race days). Pass Southdown and Susse stands and then the gates and taxi drop off point. Walk on. Pass the racecourse stat canteen. Walk straight on up past a waymarker signpost and along the footpat which runs between a flint wall and the racecourse.

2 Where the footpath hits a bridleway, **turn right**. Almost immediately **turn left** t follow the wooden waymarked mud track down past the farm. Soon, the track open out on to a grassy field. **Walk straight ahead** and cross the stile, heading into th trees. Cross a couple of wooden bridges and follow the track left and then **round th edge of the fields**. Keep following the track **straight ahead** along the hedge toward the Downs. At the end of the hedge, pass into the next field and follow the trac **straight ahead**. At the metal gate, continue **straight ahead**. Ignore any footpath to the left and keep following the waymarked footpath **straight ahead** toward Plumpton College and the Downs.

3 Pass through Plumpton Agricultural College buildings and car park. After the bric gate posts, and shortly before you reach the main road, **go left** through the gates to follow the grassy public footpath between two fences. Go through the gate and wall **diagonally right** across the field to the top corner. Arrive by the front garden of the Half Moon.

> ✪ **SC**: To miss out the downland loop and return to Plumpton Green across fields go straight to point 10.

4 Cross the road in front of the pub and follow the wooden bridleway sign **straight ahead** along the wide mud track up on to the Downs. At the top, the path forks. **Take the right fork**, following the blue marker post straight ahead along the South Downs Way (SDW) for a short distance.

5 At the gate, just before the lane, **turn left** following the marked bridleway. Pass a marker post on the path, then farm buildings and a bungalow on your right. Go through the gate and **walk right** to the stile. Cross it and follow the footpath left. Pass the barn and cross another stile into the next field. Walk on **straight ahead**, staying on the footpath. Look out for the marker post. Head **diagonally right** across the field. See Ditchling Beacon car park off to your right. Cross the stile and continue **straight ahead** across the field to the gate. Go through the gate and follow the bridleway straight ahead down the slope. Pass the marker post. Follow the path down and along the fence. Go through the gate and again follow the path along the fence which runs alongside the copse. The ground rises to your left. Go through the wooden gate and follow the bridleway into the trees. Enjoy the welcome shade and keep climbing until you find yourself at a crossroads with a carved tree trunk.

6 **Walk right** along the bridleway through broadleaf woodland. After some time, notice the flint wall to your right. Follow the waymarked bridleway straight ahead at the sign. As you approach the road, the path forks. Follow the bridleway **right**.

7 Cross Ditchling Road and go through the gate opposite to follow the bridleway **straight ahead**. The path descends and goes right to pass this field of rapeseed. Go through the gate and follow on what is now a mud bridleway across the top edge of the field. This path leads to Ditchling Beacon. Follow the chalk bridleway up the steep hill. Go through the gate and follow the path straight ahead between the fences. The chalk path opens up into a field. Keep straight ahead towards the gate. Go through and walk on until you hit the SDW. Go through the gate.

8 **Turn right** and join the SDW, heading towards Ditchling Beacon. Go through the gate and car park. Cross the road and go through the gate. Follow the SDW **straight ahead** along the ridge. Go through the gate and cross the small lane. Follow the SDW **straight ahead**. Soon, you will recognise the path from earlier and as Plumpton College comes into view, you're back at the curve in the bridleway.

9 **Head left**, back down Plumpton Bostall and across the road to the pub.

DIRECTIONS CONTINUE OVERLEAF

Directions – Agricultural Weald, Pubs & Downland to Ditchling Beacon continued...

10 **Go along Plumpton Lane**. It's to the right of the pub but can also be reached by turning left out of the pub garden. Very soon, after the bus stop, **go right** across the stile, leaving the road to join the footpath. Head for the gate with the yellow arrow and straight on to another stile. **Walk left** for a short distance, **then right** across the steps. Head across the field towards the top edge of the trees. Go over a makeshift stile. Follow the path **straight ahead** along the edge of the trees. Walk through the gap into the next field and follow the path **left** beside the hedge. Cross the drive to the house and follow the wooden waymarked footpath diagonally right across the field. Cross the stile and the small lane and go through the kissing gate opposite. Walk straight ahead.

11 You are on Novington Lane. **Turn left** briefly then **turn right** to follow the public footpath up the concrete driveway and through Warningore farmyard. Pass a house, following the bridleway **left**. **Keep left** and go through the gateway. After a couple of fields, the path forks and you must choose **the right gateway**, following the small blue arrow on the left gatepost. Walk along the side of the field to the small bridleway-marked gatepost. Go through it. **Head right** and through the metal gate. Walk on straight ahead through two more metal gates. The chalky path narrows as it climbs slightly. At the red brick house 'The Grange' **turn left** to follow the long concrete track, which is a public footpath.

12 Cross the road and climb over the stile. Walk **diagonally right** across the field until you hit another stile. Emerge on the lane in East Chiltington.

13 **Go left** and pass The Jolly Sportsman pub. **Turn left** for a short stretch on the lane into East Chiltington. By the church, follow the wide bridleway **right**. Cross the bridge over the stream. **Turn right** through the gateway and immediately walk **left** across the bridge on a footpath. Head **right** along the edge of the field. The footpath diverts briefly into grazing fields to cross five stiles. Continue round the field. Go through the wide gap into the next field. **Turn left** towards the railway line. See the marker point just before the crossing. On the other side of the railway line, **turn left** and follow the railway line back to Plumpton Green past the recreation ground.

Alternative way back from East Chiltington:
Almost opposite the pub, **turn right** on to the footpath which is signed on the telephone pole next to Chapel Cottages. Go through rustic gate and **straight ahead** on to the track, following the footpath through the five-bar gate. Walk through another gate, heading diagonally across to the stile. Now you are in a larger field. The official path leads **straight ahead** across the crops. However, it may be more prudent to take the clearer path running **diagonally left and then follow the track right** as it runs between the edge of the field and the copse. At the far end of the copse/field, the railway crossing is on your left. **Use the railway crossing and turn left** to follow the railway line all the way back to Plumpton Green past the recreation ground.

THE DOWNS NEAR DITCHLING BEACON

VISTAS OVER LEWES RAPE

DISTANCE: 14.5KM/9MILES » **TOTAL ASCENT:** 282M/925FT » **START GR:** TQ 423053 » **TIME:** ALLOW 4.5 HOURS
SATNAV: BN7 3HX » **MAP:** OS EXPLORER OL11, BRIGHTON & HOVE, 1:25,000 » **REFRESHMENTS:** THE JUGGS, KINGSTON, OR
THE ABERGAVENNY ARMS, RODMELL » **NAVIGATION:** CARE NEEDED IN IFORD TO SPOT STILE AT POINT 9.

17 Vistas over Lewes Rape: Country Pubs, Distinctive Churches & Virginia Woolf's Stomping Ground

14.5km/9miles

A sharp climb up to a downland ridge that offers extensive views from coast to castle, passing a top pub in Kingston before meandering through agricultural fields to Rodmell, home of Virginia Woolf, and a triumphant return along the River Ouse to peaceful Southease.

Southease » Mill Hill » Front Hill » Hard Hill » Swanborough Hill » Kingston near Lewes » Swanborough » Iford » Rodmell » River Ouse » Southease

Start

Roadside parking by Southease Church, accessible from lane off Kingston Road between Lewes and Newhaven. GR: TQ 423053.

The Walk

Pick up the South Downs Way in the peaceful hamlet of Southease. Southease church is one of only three churches in Sussex to have a round tower. The thirteenth century flint tower and wall paintings are significant, as perhaps once the village was: Southease is recorded in the Domesday book as having a thriving herring fishing industry.

This is a stunning stretch of the South Downs Way running along the ridge through rolling agricultural downland with ever-changing and exhilarating vistas over what was once the Norman 'rape' or district of Lewes. The views to the sea, over open fields, and on towards Sussex villages and Lewes town put life into perspective.

Descend to Swanborough or head on to Kingston with its fourteenth century church and the much-loved Juggs pub. The pub is named after the fish baskets carried by Newhaven fishwives on their way to market in Lewes. This friendly pub offers log fires, a cheerful terrace and garden, bustling atmosphere and good food.

Footpaths lead you on through crop fields, past barns and grazing horses. You never quite know when you're going to turn a corner and find a field of wild flowers basking in the reflected glory of the Downs.

The Abergavenny Arms in Rodmell is a traditional and welcoming pub with well-kept Harvey's beer and a frequently changing menu. Rodmell is also home to an eighteenth century weather-boarded cottage called Monk's House. This was the country retreat of Virginia and Leonard Woolf. Virginia was inspired by the Sussex countryside for over two decades but tragically committed suicide by drowning in the River Ouse. It's possible to visit the room where Woolf created some of her best works. The National Trust house is open on certain days only (check online for details) when the local pub may fortuitously be offering cream teas.

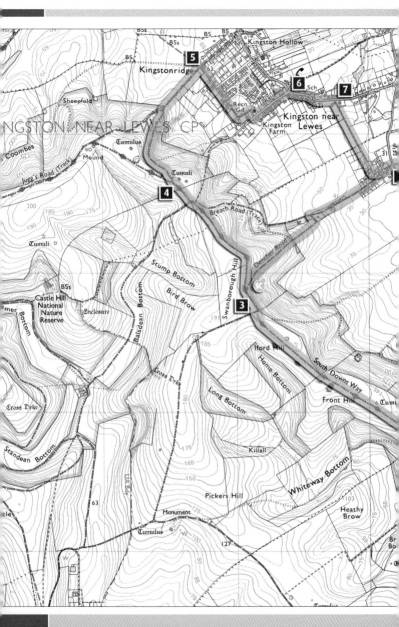

**17 VISTAS OVER
LEWES RAPE**

Directions – Vistas over Lewes Rape

➔ Pick up the South Downs Way (SDW) to walk up the lane to the top of the hill, passing to the right of the church. At the main road, **go right** to follow the SDW along the roadside. **Cross the road** and Gorham's Lane opposite, to go through the gate. Follow the clearly marked SDW across the field and then on to a track and through a second gate. **Turn left** by the signpost of the fence to walk along the hard-surfaced track.

2 **Turn right**, before the farm buildings, to **follow the SDW**. **Go right** through a gate and climb up a hill, still following the SDW. Go through a gate, cross the lane and follow the narrow path straight ahead running alongside the fence. At the end, go through a gate and follow the SDW **straight ahead** through agricultural downland crossing a byway through more gates by a signpost. **Continue straight on**. Pass through a gate and continue **straight ahead** on a long concrete bridleway through crop fields. **Easy to miss:** at the top of the slope, near the signpost, where the concrete path turns sharp left, **follow the grassy SDW right**. Follow the path as it **curves left through a gate**, running along Swanborough Hill.

3 At the signpost, you have a choice:

   ⟿ **SC: Take the right fork**, sweeping down towards Swanborough along 'Dencher Road'. Follow the bridleway through the gate and then at the bottom of the hill follow the marker posts as the track veers **left**. **Walk right** at the junction with the bridleway in the trees. The path turns into a concrete lane, running between houses. It rejoins the main route just before point 8 as it passes the marker post and Swanborough Manor.

To continue on our main route to Kingston (and pub!), follow the stony bridleway as it curves round to the left then **straight ahead**. (Fabulous vistas!) Walk along the flint bridleway then across the field. Pass a signpost and go through a gate.

4 At the signpost, **turn right**, leaving the SDW to head down the hill into Kingston. Take care: the compacted chalk may be slippery.

5 At the bottom of the hill, **turn right past two low wooden bollards** down the tarmac track. Continue along Church Lane. **Keep straight ahead at the recreation ground** and walk past the tennis court. At the corner, **follow the tarmac path left**

Beside the flint church, **turn right along the tarmac path**. Go through the gate and **turn left along the lane**.

6 Pass The Juggs pub and reach the road junction. Cross the road to walk on the pavement and **turn right towards Newhaven along Ashcombe Lane**. Pass the school and some houses.

7 Just after the *20 mph zone* sign, see the marker post on the far side of the road. **Turn right**, crossing the road to follow the narrow, signed footpath. Go through a gate and walk on. Go through a further gate and **walk straight ahead** through the farm buildings. Once through the farm, **veer left** on the track. **Walk straight ahead** past Swanborough Manor.

8 At the road, cross and **go straight ahead through a gate**. Follow the not obvious footpath across the field. See Lewes Castle to your left. **Turn right** at the marker post and walk in a straight line to the wooden fenced opening. Go through the opening and follow the path straight ahead. In the corner of the field, to the right of the metal gate,

DIRECTIONS CONTINUE OVERLEAF

KINGSTON CHURCH

there is a stile. Follow the path straight ahead. Go over a stile and **turn right** in order to continue straight ahead towards the lane. Cross the lane, go over the stile and walk beside the flint wall and hedge. Go through a gate, cross the drive to Iford Manor, and through another gate, **continuing straight ahead**. Go through a metal kissing gate.

9 Go left to follow the lane a very short distance to the corner of a wall. **Turn right through an open gate by an easy-to-miss disused stile and then turn left to keep walking in the same direction on the footpath**, (passing a cottage on your left) and on through the crop field and then straight on through next field of crops. At the bridleway, take a few steps right.

10 At the road, **take care and turn left** to follow it for a good 5 minutes.

11 Just after you leave Northease, at the metal gates, beyond Whiteway House, look for a signpost and footpath and **head left** leaving the road. Pass by the post and **follow the footpath straight ahead** through what appears to be a large back garden. Pass beside the tennis courts, over the stone steps and **straight ahead**. Go through the 'pinch' gate and along the footpath to the lane.

12 You are now in Rodmell.

OR **Go right** to find the Abergavenny Arms up the lane.

Go left to continue on the main route past Monk's House. Stay on the lane until you pass the car park. Continue straight ahead, passing a stream and following the public bridleway. Go through a metal gate. Pass a post and walk for a while. See Mount Caburn ahead. Go through another couple of gates and continue on.

13 At the river bank, **walk right**, through the kissing gate to follow the footpath along the riverbank. Walk through the kissing gate and continue on. See Southease Church spire to your right. Go through the gate at Southease Bridge.

14 **Turn right** to return to Southease church along the SDW, or **turn left** over the bridge for Southease Station.

WILD FLOWERS IN CROP FIELD NEAR IFORD

FROM VILLAGES TO BEACONS, RIDGES TO COACH ROADS

DISTANCE: 13.3KM/8.3MILES » **TOTAL ASCENT:** 361M/1,184FT » **START GR:** TQ 520051 » **TIME:** ALLOW 5 HOURS
SATNAV: BN26 6SP » **MAP:** OS EXPLORER OL25, EASTBOURNE & BEACHY HEAD, 1:25,000 » **REFRESHMENTS:** THE CRICKETERS
ARMS, BERWICK; VARIOUS PUBS AND TEAROOMS IN ALFRISTON; THE RAM INN; FIRLE » **NAVIGATION:** STRAIGHTFORWARD.

VIEW FROM NEAR FIRLE BEACON

18 From Villages to Beacons, Ridges to Coach Roads

13.3km/8.3miles

From the historic villages of Berwick and Alfriston, make an exhilarating ridge-top trek to Firle Beacon, walking back past Charleston (Bloomsbury set!) on the old coach track.

Berwick » Alfriston » Bostal Hill » Firle Beacon » Charleston Farmhouse » Alciston » Berwick

Start

Public car park opposite The Cricketers Arms. GR: TQ 520051.

The Walk

This exhilarating walk can be adapted to suit each individual. Some may prefer to explore the picturesque villages in a shorter route while hardened walkers will enjoy the chance to gather speed on the old coach road. The ridge top South Downs Way trek with its expansive views is highly recommended.

Choose from two characterful real ale pubs: The Cricketers Arms in picturesque Berwick, or The Ram Inn at Firle. Visit Berwick Church, where colourful frescoes on the walls and pulpit contrast with simple side windows. Follow our optional route through Alfriston, where flint and Tudor buildings house an eclectic selection of independent shops, tearooms and pubs.

As you walk across crop fields on Vanguard Way, look towards the Downs. Seeing where you've been or where you're heading to on a walk is a great way of bringing landscape, and our own place in it, into perspective. Later, from up high, the views are far-reaching: spot Lullington Heath or look left to where the sea lurks and glimmers beyond grazing sheep.

At 217 metres, Firle Beacon is one of the highest points on the South Downs Way. It remains unspoilt, perhaps because the car park necessitates a short walk. There are extensive views over Mount Caburn and the Lewes Downs. Look for the roof of Glyndebourne Opera House.

The tracks in this area are historically well-trodden and increasingly well-signed since the advent of the South Downs National Park. English Heritage list Roman round barrows near Bopeep chalk pit, Bopeep Bostal and Firle Beacon. The mound beside the trig point at Firle Beacon is what remains of a Roman long barrow. During summer, detour to artistic Charleston, home and country meeting place of the Bloomsbury Group. Walking along the old coach road gives you some sense of journeys travelled on foot in the past. Are you sure those are only your own footsteps that you can hear?

18 FROM VILLAGES TO BEACONS, RIDGES TO COACH ROADS

⑤ From the car park, continue along the tarmac lane heading away from the main road. At the mini roundabout, **turn left** towards Berwick Church. At the signpost, walk **diagonally left** to climb over a stile. Walk along the fence and pop into the church. Otherwise continue along the hedge and **turn right**. Go through a kissing gate and arrive at crop fields beside the churchyard. Take a few steps **right**.

2 **At the marker post, turn left** along the footpath perpendicular to the church. You are on Vanguard Way. Follow this track to Alfriston, with the Downs and a distant Firle Beacon on your right. Climb a slope, pass a marker post and take a few steps along a shingle track.

3 At the signpost and crossroads, you have a choice:

To head directly up on to the Downs, possibly with a less steep climb, **walk right** at the wooden waymarker post to follow the bridleway. Where the paths fork, take the middle track. At the next fork, **keep left**, going **straight ahead**, up the rather steep hill to the top.

> **OR** Walk **straight ahead** to divert through the village of Alfriston. At the lane you actually have a further choice: either **walk straight ahead** along the lane with its steady trickle of cars, **OR turn left** down the lane, then **right** along the public footpath just after Winton Barn. Follow this past some houses, over a stile, straight ahead across a field and over another stile. The views are good but the last stretch runs behind gardens and can be overgrown. Rejoin the lane and **turn left**.
>
> Follow Vanguard Way along the lane into Alfriston. Walk through the village centre along the High Street. Pass Rope Walk. **Turn right** into Star Lane, following the South Downs Way (SDW). Cross Weaver's Lane and follow the SDW **straight ahead**. Walk past the houses. Just after 'The Broadway', the road changes into an unmade track. Climb up following the SDW. Just before West Down, **walk right** on the bridleway. At the end, **turn left** to climb up this steep track. This is possibly the steepest but shadiest climb. **Turn left** on to the bridleway as you approach the top and the SDW. Or, on a winter's day, you may prefer to walk **straight ahead** at West Down, heading upwards on the hard-surfaced SDW to the top where it turns right, rejoining our main route at point 4.

4 **Turn right** through the gate to join the SDW. After the gateway, the views open out to your right and you can see Arlington Reservoir.

5 At the marker post, Green Way bridleway crosses your path. **Stay straight ahead** on the SDW.

  SC: Turn diagonally right at the five-way signpost to take a bridleway down Bostal Hill. **Turn right** on to the lane, rejoining the main route to **turn right** by Bopeep Farmhouse on to the old coach road and byway at point 9.

Continue along the SDW. Pass the car park at Bopeep disused chalk pit.

6 At the marker post, go **straight ahead**.

  SC: Turn right on to the bridleway, which joins the old coach road. **Turn right** on to the byway, rejoining the main route at point 8.

Walk onwards and reach Firle Beacon with its OS marker, and views out over Mount Caburn and the Lewes Downs. At the marker post, leave the SDW and **take the course leading right**. The bridleway is not obvious, but keep straight ahead, aiming for the spur which leads down to the trees and the white, perpendicular path below. Take the chalk track leading down before you reach the spur. Follow the meandering path which, thankfully, is not as steep as it initially appears. Go through the gate and **straight ahead** across the field.

DIRECTIONS CONTINUE OVERLEAF

Directions – From Villages to Beacons, Ridges to Coach Roads continued...

7 Emerge through a gateway on to the old coach track (byway). **Walk right** on this muc and flint bridleway. Stay on this track, ignoring the bridleway shooting off left.

> ⟩OR⟩ **Head left** on the old coach track, following the track into Firle village where you will find The Ram Inn.

Walk on this easy and fast byway all the way back to Alciston. Notice Firle Tower **Keep right** at the house where the private road is marked.

8 **Walk straight ahead**, past the bridleway going left to Tilton Farm. There is a track going right here that is the bridleway in the shortcut in point 6 above.

> ⟩OR⟩ To visit Charleston Farmhouse, meeting place of the Bloomsbury Group **go left** on the bridleway and follow it down to the houses and barn. After about 500m, the bridleway turns into a concrete track that bends to the left On your right is a driveway to Tilton House. At the end of the concrete track look for a sign, announcing *Charleston* and a track on the left, leading up to Charleston. Follow this track and soon, you'll arrive at Charleston, with the pond on the right and the visitor entrance on the left.

Pass the old house and flint barn (Upper Barn) on Firle Estate.

9 Cross the road by the Bopeep Farmhouse B&B. This is where the shortcut in point 5 descends. Walk straight ahead on the byway. Pass a footpath heading right.

10 At the seat signed for Alciston, **walk left**. The path joins the road briefly. After the flint buildings and the wall, **go right through a gap in the hedge** on an unsigned footpath which initially runs parallel with the road and past a sand school. At the hedge and marker post, **turn right** on the footpath alongside the hedge towards Berwick Church. At the bridleway marker post, **turn left**. At the post in the corner of the field, **turn right** and follow the path into Berwick where it joins a concrete track At the mini-roundabout, **go left** back to the pub and car park.

BETWEEN BERWICK AND ALFRISTON

A FAVOURITE WALK

DISTANCE: 22.6KM/14MILES » **TOTAL ASCENT:** 696M/2,282FT » **START GR:** TQ 518002 » **TIME:** ALLOW 7-8 HOURS
SATNAV: BN25 4AJ » **MAP:** OS EXPLORER OL25, EASTBOURNE & BEACHY HEAD, 1:25,000 » **REFRESHMENTS:** THE PLOUGH
AND HARROW OR LITLINGTON TEA GARDENS, LITLINGTON; THE EIGHT BELLS OR JEVINGTON TEA GARDENS, JEVINGTON; TIGER
INN, EAST DEAN (OPTIONAL ROUTE); NATIONAL TRUST CAFE, BIRLING GAP; SALTMARSH FARMHOUSE CAFE, EXCEAT; THE
CUCKMERE INN, EXCEAT BRIDGE » **NAVIGATION:** MAINLY STRAIGHTFORWARD. PATHS IN THE CROWLINK NATIONAL TRUST
AREA ARE ON OPEN ACCESS LAND AND NOT NECESSARILY OBVIOUS OR SIGNED.

LULLINGTON HEATH

19 A Favourite Walk: Forest, Heath, Downland & Chalk Cliff

22.6km/14miles

A loop which leads you through forest, heath and downland, culminating in the spectacular Seven Sisters cliff path.

Friston Forest » Litlington » Lullington Heath » Jevington » Willingdon Hill » East Dean » Birling Gap » Seven Sisters » Exceat » Friston Forest

Start

Litlington Road car park (parking charge), off the minor road between Exceat and Litlington. GR: TQ 518002.

The Walk

This circuit is both demanding and satisfying. The paths used are the well-established tracks so often favoured by long distance walkers. The magnificent terrain includes forest, downland, heath and coast, plus a couple of significant climbs. Views are spectacular and guaranteed to lift your spirits. Start in tranquil Friston Forest, passing Charleston Manor, home of painter Sir Oswald Birley and 'heritage' garden designer Lady Rhoda. Look out for Clapham House, 'love-nest' of Mrs Elizabeth Fitzherbert who secretly married the Prince Regent, later George IV, in 1746. Litlington also boasts a good pub and nostalgic tea gardens.

Climb to the dewpond and walk on through Lullington Heath National Nature Reserve. Follow this undulating chalk track though a colourful patchwork of mixed scrub, chalk grasslands and the best remaining example of chalk heath in Britain. The Eight Bells,

with its pleasant garden, is a firm favourite with walkers. It's a steep climb out of Jevington but reaching the crest of the ridge and seeing the English Channel is a highlight of the walk. Some say that you can see France on a clear day!

Crowlink and Seven Sisters are sheep grazing, cliff-walking country, notorious for both smuggling and erosion. Detour to the National Trust coffee shop, bar, beach and coastguard cottages at Birling Gap. The undulating cliffs are always memorable as each 'sister' is unique: from the East, count Went Hill Brow (45m), Baily's Brow (60m), Flagstaff Point (47m), Brass Point (50m), Rough Brow (67m), Short Brow (78m). Flat Brow, between Baily's Brow and Flagstaff Point, is the disregarded eighth sister. The meandering river at Cuckmere snakes across the valley floor, hinting at oxbow lake potential. This walk was designed by my father, Bob Huston, who counts this area as one of his preferred walking haunts and professes this particular walk to be his ideal circuit. Judge for yourself. I think you'll enjoy it. I know I do.

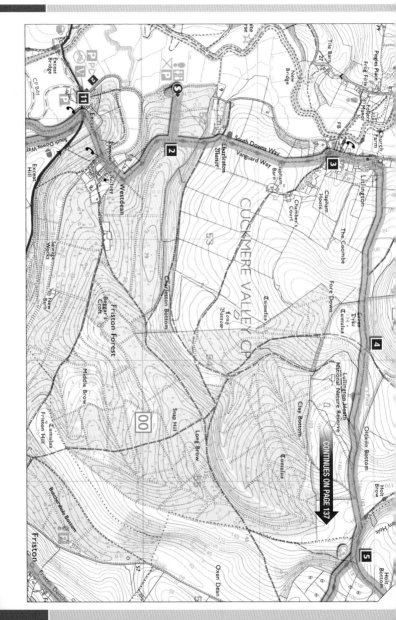

CONTINUES ON PAGE 137

STARTS ON PAGE 136

CONTINUES ON PAGE 139

19 A FAVOURITE WALK

Directions – A Favourite Walk

➎ Locate the forest track on the far left-hand side of the car park, behind the climbing wall structure. Follow the sign for White Horse View, in order to join the South Downs Way (SDW) and, at the fork just beyond the climbing structure, **take the right path**. At the top of a moderate climb, note the bench as a landmark for your return and hit the flat grassy SDW.

2 **Turn left**, following the SDW. Walk on between two fence posts and down some steep steps. Continue along the SDW as it curves past a flint barn in the grounds of Charleston Manor. **Turn right** and climb over a stile to stay on the SDW. Walk up this steepish path beside a hedge. Glimpse the White Horse to your left. Near the top, climb over a stile and walk on along the side of a hedge enjoying the feeling of being elevated on the Downs. On your right, see distant Clapham House. Go through a kissing gate to continue straight ahead. Go through another kissing gate to descend into Litlington. Be careful by the second kissing gate: it's slippery! **Turn left** on to the lane.

3 **Turn right** on to the road and pass the Plough and Harrow. Ignore the SDW as it veers left and **walk straight ahead on the road**. Pass Litlington Tea Gardens. Just beyond St Michael's Church, **turn right** to follow the wide concrete bridleway. Pass the old barn with circular pillars and **turn left** along the bridleway. Follow this bridleway as it climbs to the top.

4 Pass Winchester's Pond and **walk straight ahead** on the undulating bridleway through Lullington Heath Nature Reserve. Leave the heath and at the bridleway marker post, **follow the SDW straight ahead**. The path leads you through a wood.

5 At the fork, by the SDW sign, you have a choice:

> ◔ **SC: Go right** on the bridleway SDW to bypass the village, rejoining the main route by the churchyard at point 6.

To follow the main route, go straight ahead for the pub and follow the bridleway into Jevington village. At Green Lane, opposite the Old Post Office, **turn right** along the road to reach The Eight Bells pub. Continue along the road. Follow the footpath waymarker along the pavement as it leads you **right** alongside a flint wall and on through a gated churchyard.

DIRECTIONS CONTINUE OVERLEAF

CONTINUES ON PAGE 136

19 A FAVOURITE WALK

Directions – A Favourite Walk continued...

6 Turn left out of the churchyard down the lane. **Turn right at the road**, past the bus stop. Pass Jevington Tea Gardens. **Take the second left into Eastbourne Lane**, following the SDW sign to climb out of Jevington.

7 Enjoy the far-reaching views at the ridge. **Walk right along the ridge**. Go through a gate and follow the bridleway. Pass a sheep shearing station to your left. Enjoy the downhill stretch as you descend Willingdon Hill. Go through the gate and keep following the bridleway down, now with views over the sea and Friston Forest. **Turn right**, following the path as it runs alongside the fence. **Keep straight ahead**, ignoring the first bridleway to East Dean. At the gate, hit a bridleway and **turn left**. The track turns into residential Willingdon Road. Pass the water tower.

8 At the triangle of grass at the end of Old Willingdon Rd, you have a choice:

> **OR** **Cross the A259**. **Turn left**, following the footpath which runs alongside the A259 to reach the Tiger Inn at East Dean. Retrace steps to join main route.

To follow the main route to the coast, cross the A259, **bearing left** and go **straight ahead**, heading down Crowlink Lane past the church. Pass Crowlink National Trust car park. At the gate, just before the National Trust Crowlink notice, **turn left and head diagonally across the field** towards the sea and the gate in the middle of the fence. (**Note:** paths in this area are generally unsigned and not necessarily obvious.) Go through the gate and head left towards the trees. **Turn right** along the fence. Walk past the five-bar gate and at the kissing gate **turn left. Head for the barn.** Pass with the barn on your left, keeping your direction the same. Head on past the scrub and aim for the gate, once it comes into view. Go through the gate, head for the next gate ahead and continue on down the path.

9 At the signpost, **head right** for Exceat.

> **OR** **Keep straight ahead** for a small diversion to National Trust Birling Gap cafe, coastguard cottages, beach and public toilets. Rejoin the main route below, heading back across the Seven Sisters to Exceat.

Go through the gate and follow the path **straight ahead** as it undulates over the cliffs. Count the seven (plus one unofficial!) sisters and pass two memorials as you continue straight ahead across the undulating cliff peaks. At the gate, **leave Crowlink** to enter the Seven Sisters Country Park. Go through the gate and at the peak of the last sister, you should see the ever-magnificent meandering Cuckmere. Take the SDW **right** to Exceat. Go through a gate.

10 You have a choice:

> The footpath runs **straight ahead** above the valley with fabulous views and passes the site of the disappeared village of Exceat.

Go through the gate and **turn right** on to the track. Head straight ahead on the left bridleway.

11 Go through the gate. Cross the A259. **Head right**, passing to the right of the flint building (a shop for sale, at the time of writing). **Go through the kissing gate** and walk up the grazing field on the trodden grass footpath. It's a steepish climb but offers a viewpoint over the spectacular estuary. At the top, **go through the gate** and use the stone step to **climb over the flint wall**. After a couple of steps to the right, **continue straight ahead** along the SDW past a marker post and down lots of steps. **Pass the pond** in the historic hamlet of Westdean. **Continue straight ahead** on the signed SDW. (At the stone marker, you may wish to detour right to visit the twelfth-century church.) Pass The Long House and The Glebe and begin to climb. Pass a signpost and gate and amble on up the wooded SDW. At the end of the fence, **turn left** along the SDW as signed. Stay on the SDW until you reach the bench, where you **turn left** for the car park.

HERITAGE COASTLINE

DISTANCE: 12KM/7.5MILES » **TOTAL ASCENT:** 451M/1,479FT » **START GR:** TV 587978 » **TIME:** ALLOW 4 HOURS
SATNAV: BN20 7XX » **MAP:** OS EXPLORER OL25, EASTBOURNE & BEACHY HEAD, 1:25,000 » **REFRESHMENTS:** THE BEACHY
HEAD, BEACHY HEAD; SEASONAL SNACK KIOSK, BELLE TOUT; NATIONAL TRUST CAFE, BIRLING GAP; TIGER INN, HIKER'S REST OR
BEEHIVE ON THE GREEN, EAST DEAN (OPTIONAL ROUTE) » **NAVIGATION:** STRAIGHTFORWARD EXCEPT AT WEALD WAY, WHERE
TAKING THE WRONG PATH LEADS TO A STEEP DESCENT WITH AN EQUALLY STEEP CLIMB BACK UP: SEE OPTIONAL ROUTE.
EASTBOURNE DOWNLAND (EXCEPT FOR FARMLAND) IS OPEN ACCESS AND THERE MAY NOT ALWAYS BE AN 'OBVIOUS' PATH.

BEACHY HEAD LIGHTHOUSE

Heritage Coastline: Beachy Head, Belle Tout & Farmed Downland

12km/7.5miles

An exhilarating walk along the chalk cliffs with views over Eastbourne, downland and the channel, plus the chance to see Beachy Head and Belle Tout lighthouses, before returning across farmland.

Warren Hill » Weald Way » Beachy Head » Belle Tout » Birling Gap » Wigden's Bottom » Crapham Bottom » Warren Hill

Start

Warren Hill car park (parking charge) is on the B2103. From the A259, turn on to the B2103. The car park is on the left before the turn off to Beachy Head. GR: TV 587978.

The Walk

Walking along a cliff edge is strangely appealing, made doubly so by the largely undeveloped nature of this, the first ever designated Heritage Coastline, a spectacular area of natural beauty. Erosion is a constant factor at play here from the whitening of the cliffs to the destruction of coastguard cottages at Birling Gap.

This is Eastbourne Downland – rare chalk grassland and home to a rich variety of plants, insects and birds. Plants, such as downland orchids, thrive on the springy turf which is a consequence of thin, poor soil, slow-growing plants and a history of sheep-grazing. The chalk cliffs, channel-side location, abundance of gorse and autumn berries all make this a desirable area for a wide variety of birds to live in and stop by. Even the peregrine falcon has returned to nest here during the last decade!

At 162 metres, Beachy Head is the highest chalk sea cliff in Britain but the views are such that you may forgive the uphill gradients. On a clear day, you can see Dungeness in Kent, or as far west as Selsey Bill and the Isle of Wight. The iconic red and white Beachy Head lighthouse stands beneath the cliffs and whilst no longer manned, is still fully functional. Belle Tout, however, is now an unusual B&B with a seasonal refreshment kiosk. Belle Tout lighthouse was built in 1832 but decommissioned in 1902 because erosion had altered its position. In 1999, the building was moved seventeen metres back from the cliff edge in an attempt to save it from the ravages of erosion. The very busy National Trust cafe at Birling gap is open all day.

This stretch of coastline is deservedly popular. The second part of the walk across farmland is quiet in contrast. If your timings work, it's easy to follow our optional route to East Dean where a couple of cafes and the Tiger Inn offer a choice of refreshments.

BELLE TOUT

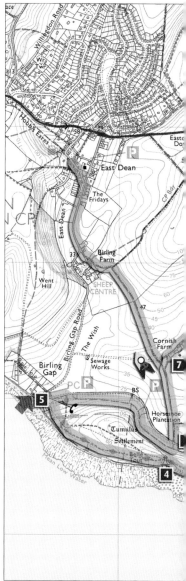

20 HERITAGE COASTLINE

Directions – Heritage Coastline

Be aware of danger from STEEP drops and erosion at cliff edges.

↱ Spot a signpost just north of the car park and join a grassy bridleway towards Willingdon / Eastbourne and some trees. Enjoy views over the sea. At the signpost **turn right** along the grassy South Downs Way (SDW), doubling back towards the road on a mud track through copse and scrub.

2 The SDW passes by the road junction for Birling Gap. Walk across the B2103, as signed, and walk left and up the slope and left again to **continue on the well-signed SDW**. As you near the sea, spy a signpost in a patch of scrub and **turn left** down the hill on the SDW towards the sea and Eastbourne. Continue down the slope on the SDW past another signpost.

3 At the next marker post, take care. Ignore the 'straight ahead' arrow on the post and go **diagonally right** to pick up the SDW; here it is a chalk track heading between bushes. At the top of the hill, pass a SDW signpost and **curve left** towards the sea to stay on the footpath. **Pass a marker post**. Continue on. By a marker post, the SDW joins a tarmac path. **Pass a memorial** to RAF Bomber Command. For maximum safety, stay on the tarmac track until in sight of the Vintage Inn then veer left across the grass and past a marker post. **Walk along the undulating cliff top** to the lighthouse. You pass Beachy Head Lighthouse but at this point, it's out of sight. Look back and at some point you'll be rewarded with a view of the lighthouse and cliffs.

4 Reach Belle Tout Lighthouse and seasonal snack bar. Continue on. Go down the path and steps to Birling Gap car park.

5 Reach Birling Gap with National Trust cafe and bar, public toilets, beach and abandoned coastguard cottages. To continue with your walk, turn right through the car park. Pass opposite a bus stop and signpost and continue along the grassy bridleway. briefly onto the road. At the wooden waymarker, **follow the bridleway** (not the SDW) **diagonally right**.

6 Look out for the signpost at the start of a concrete track on the far side of the road, level with Belle Tout lighthouse, which is up and out of sight behind you. **Turn left** and cross the road, following the bridleway round the gate and straight ahead towards East Dean Down. At the first signpost, keep **straight ahead** towards East Dean.

7 Where the concrete track curves towards the farm, stay on the bridleway as it **curves right**.

> OR Leave the concrete track to **walk straight ahead** on the grassy path. Pass the marker post and go through the gate. **Walk straight ahead** towards East Dean and the pub. **Go left** at the next bridleway junction to go behind the sheep centre and **walk right** along the Birling Gap Road. **At East Dean, follow the minor road left** to find the Tiger Inn.

Turn right to pass Cornish Farm. Go through the gate to the left of the barn and walk on. Pass a signpost then a red-tiled house. At the wooden waymarker signpost, **walk straight ahead** towards Warren Hill on the bridleway. Go through the gate and follow the line of the fence towards a small building. Go through a gate.

8 By the dewpond and small building **walk left** through the gate on the bridleway. Walk on and through another gate. Walk up the hill, along the line of the fence. Go through the gate and **turn right** along the road. You will soon reach Warren Hill car park.

Appendix

Tourist Information Centres

www.southdowns.gov.uk – Official website for the National Park.

Brighton	T: 01273 290 337
Burgess Hill	T: 01444 238 202
Chichester	T: 01243 950 412
Eastbourne	T: 01323 415 415
Lewes	T: 01273 483 448
Midhurst	T: 01730 814 810
Petersfield	T: 01730 268 829
Seaford	T: 01323 897 426
Winchester	T: 01962 840 500
Worthing	T: 01903 221 066

Food and Drink
Cafes

See individual routes for recommendations.

Wildflour Cafe, Saddlescombe Farm	T: (no telephone)
Jevington Tea Gardens	T: 01323 489 682
Saltmarsh Farmhouse Cafe, Exceat	T: 01323 870 218
Litlington Tea Gardens	T: 01323 870 222
Amberley Village Tea Room	T: 01798 839 196
The Purple Carrot at No6, Hassocks	T: 07763 641 879

Pubs

See individual routes for recommendations.

The Milbury's, Beauworth	T: 01962 771 248
The George, Burpham	T: 01903 883 131
The Labouring Man, Coldwaltham	T: 01798 873 337
The Shepherd and Dog, Fulking	T: 01273 857 38?
The Eight Bells, Jevington	T: 01323 484 44?
Half Moon, Plumpton	T: 01273 890 25?
The White Horse, Sutton	T: 01798 869 19?

Accommodation
Youth Hostels

YHA Youth Hostels can be found in the following places. For more information please visit www.yha.org.uk

Brighton	T: 0345 371 917?
Eastbourne	T: 0345 371 931?
Littlehampton	T: 0345 371 967?
South Downs	T: 0345 371 957?
Truleigh Hill	T: 0345 371 904?

Bunkhouses, B&Bs and Hotels

Waydown Shepherds Huts, Pyecombe	T: 07885 360 36?
South Downs Way B&B, Poynings	T: 01273 857 22?

Camping

Blackberry Wood, Streat	T: 01273 890 03?
Slindon Camping and Caravanning Club Site, Arundel	T: 01243 814 38?
Graffam Camping and Caravanning Club Site, Great Bury	T: 01798 867 47?
Holden Farm, Cheriton	T: 07599 553 74?

Weather

www.metoffice.gov.uk
www.metcheck.com

Outdoor Shops

The Outdoor Shop – Lewes
www.outdoorshoplewes.co.uk   T: 01273 487 840

Cotswold Outdoor – Brighton
www.cotswoldoutdoor.com   T: 01273 821 452

Outdoor Life – Eastbourne   T: 01323 725 372

Cotswold Outdoor – Southhampton
www.cotswoldoutdoor.com   T: 01489 799 555

Other Publications

Cycling Days Out – South East England
Deirdre Huston, Vertebrate Publishing
www.v-publishing.co.uk

Cycling in Sussex
Deirdre Huston and Marina Bullivant,
Vertebrate Publishing
www.v-publishing.co.uk

A Companion on the South Downs Way
Peter Anderson and Terry Owen,
Per-Rambulations
A detailed reference full of numerous interesting
facts about places you will pass on the SDW.
www.per-rambulations.co.uk

Day Walks on the High Weald
Deirdre Huston, Vertebrate Publishing
www.v-publishing.co.uk

Sussex Walks
Deirdre Huston, Vertebrate Publishing
www.v-publishing.co.uk

About the Author

Deirdre Huston is an author and photographer whose work is inspired by a love of history and the outdoors. Born in Crawley, she now lives beside the South Downs in Sussex with her husband and grown-up children. She is the walks writer for *Sussex Life* magazine and Assistant Editor of *Hassocks Life* magazine. In partnership with National Trust South Downs, she has made films to explore local history at ancient Saddlescombe Farm, Devil's Dyke and Cissbury Ring. She is a graduate of the MA in Creative Writing at Bath Spa University and also writes fiction. She co-authored *Cycling in Sussex*, her first guidebook for Vertebrate Publishing, back in 2008. Her other guidebooks include *Sussex Walks*, *Day Walks on the High Weald* and *Cycling Days Out – South East England*.

Vertebrate Publishing

At Vertebrate Publishing we publish books to inspire adventure. It's our rule that the only books we publish are those that we'd want to read or use ourselves. We endeavour to bring you beautiful books that stand the test of time and that you'll be proud to have on your bookshelf for years to come.
www.v-publishing.co.uk

VP DAY WALKS GUIDEBOOKS

Written by local authors, each pocket-sized guidebook features:

- 20 great day-length walks
- Ordnance Survey 1:25,000-scale maps
- easy-to-follow directions
- distance & navigation information
- refreshment stops & local area information
- detailed appendix

OS Map data

1 DAY WALKS IN THE CAIRNGORMS

2 DAY WALKS IN FORT WILLIAM & GLEN COE

3 DAY WALKS IN LOCH LOMOND & THE TROSSACHS

4 DAY WALKS IN SNOWDONIA

5 DAY WALKS IN THE BRECON BEACONS

6 DAY WALKS ON THE PEMBROKESHIRE COAST

7 DAY WALKS IN THE LAKE DISTRICT

8 DAY WALKS IN NORTHUMBERLAND

9 DAY WALKS IN THE YORKSHIRE DALES

10 DAYS WALKS IN THE NORTH YORK MOORS

11 DAY WALKS IN THE SOUTH PENNINES

12 DAY WALKS IN THE PEAK DISTRICT

13 DAY WALKS IN THE PEAK DISTRICT

14 DAY WALKS IN EAST ANGLIA

15 DAY WALKS IN THE COTSWOLDS

16 DAY WALKS IN DEVON

17 DAY WALKS ON THE HIGH WEALD

18 DAY WALKS ON THE SOUTH DOWNS

Available from book shops or direct from **www.v-publishing.co.uk**